D0131933

nine LESSONS
of successful school leadership teams

Distilling a decade of innovation

Bill McKeever and the
California School Leadership Academy

Copyright © 2003 WestEd. All rights reserved. No part of this publication may be reproduced or distributed in any form or by any means, or stored in a database or retrieval system, without the prior written permission of the publisher.

WestEd, a nonprofit research, development, and service agency, works with education and other communities to promote excellence, achieve equity, and improve learning for children, youth, and adults. While WestEd serves the states of Arizona, California, Nevada, and Utah as one of the nation's Regional Educational Laboratories, our agency's work extends throughout the United States and abroad. WestEd has 16 offices nationwide, from Washington and Boston to Arizona, Southern California, and its headquarters in San Francisco.

For more information about WestEd, visit our Web site: WestEd.org; call 415.565.3000 or toll-free, (877) 4-WestEd; or write: WestEd, 730 Harrison Street, San Francisco, CA 94107-1242.

For more information about school leadership teams and the process described in this book, contact Karen Kearney, Director of the Leadership Initiative @ WestEd, kkearne@wested.org. California School Leadership Academy (CSLA) Regional Centers can be reached through the CSLA Web site, www.csla.org.

This report was produced in whole or in part with funds from the Institute of Education Sciences, U.S. Department of Education, under contract #ED-01-CO-0012. Its contents do not necessarily reflect the views or policies of the Department of Education.

Contents

Figures

Case in Point Examples

To Suzanne Bailey

Thank you for your inspiration, your consciousness, and your coaching.

To Linda, our children, and our family

Thank you for your support, your faith, and your time.

Preface

Since our founding in 1984, the California School Leadership Academy (CSLA) has worked with hundreds of schools, in California and beyond. Over 23,000 school leaders have participated with us in exploring how to improve schools — their own schools. We have learned from them and the specifics of their situations how to improve the support we provide. They have learned from us how to work with an evolving, research-based understanding of school improvement. In this book, we hope to pass along some of this shared learning.

When school leaders work with CSLA, they undertake whole school reform. They don't come to us for speeches or checklists. They come to invest in a course of action that can be expected to take years. In fact, if we and they are successful, this course of action becomes a continuous process of school improvement. It is standard for CSLA to support school leaders through the first two or three years of this process. A key part of these experiences is the focused reflection school leaders do about how their school is changing, and why. Often, these reflections can be distilled into "lessons" that cohere over time around a few core themes. We have found the nine lessons in this book to be universally applicable for any school intent on creating a successful school leadership team.

Acknowledgments

The directors and staff of CSLA have long been involved in exploring and defining the work of school leadership teams. While the happenstance of time, location, and opportunity permits me to serve as the primary author of this book, each and every person involved in this work has contributed to the story. This book and the lessons it tells are truly the result of teamwork.

I extend my gratitude first to the visionaries, those who saw the possibility that school leadership teams could improve student achievement. These creators of the vision include Karen Kearney, Laraine Roberts, Albert Cheng, and Terry Mazany. Others have made school leadership teams a focus of their careers: Franklin Jones;

Janet H. Chrispeels; the staff of the Gervitz Graduate School of Education at the University of California, Santa Barbara; and my colleagues, the directors of CSLA's School Leadership Centers across California.

The work of the visionaries and the leaders has been supported throughout the past decade by the core staff at CSLA. Production, graphics, technological support, editing support, and administrative support have been provided by Fazela Hatef, Diana L. Lopez, Monty Martinez, Megan Shaw Prelinger, Ezra Schnick, Fred Serena, Erik Smolin, Amihan Ty, and Dan Wilson. Their efforts and creativity have helped to make the vision a reality.

Several individuals gave specific and important support to the publication process. Katherine L. Kaiser demonstrated the utmost professionalism, patience, and flexibility as editor of the book. Lynn Murphy, Freddie Baer, and Christian Holden gave the book its final structure and design. Dan Kenley, Mary Ann Sanders, Karen Dyer, and Kent Peterson were kind enough to review the text and offer support. Special thanks go to Laraine Roberts and Ellen McCarty for their contributions to the book.

Many have supported me personally. My wife, Linda McKeever, and my mother, Gladys McKeever, have continuously encouraged me to follow my passions. My children and grandchildren have inspired me and kept me focused on what is important. Dean Welin, Pam Noli, Gary Duke, Dan Kenley, Suzanne Bailey, and Karen Kearney have made significant contributions to my life as an educator and as a person. I give heartfelt thanks to each of you.

The Evolution of School Leadership

When we sent an early draft of this book to reviewers, several pointed out that we should provide more background about school leadership teams. Reviewers told us, "You've been working with school leadership teams for years, but not everyone has. Lots of people are fuzzy on the concept. Besides, your teams operate in ways that are really quite distinctive. You need to lay out how your teams work and how your vision of leadership has evolved."

What Is School Leadership?

Inspired by the profusion of effective schools research in the early 1980s, which argued for the importance of the school principal as "instructional leader," CSLA was founded at the behest of the California Legislature and the California Department of Education to help principals take on this role. It wasn't a role that had been emphasized in most principals' earlier education and training. Yet the observation by Ron Edmonds (1979) that inspired much of this interest in instructional leadership was irrefutable:

> *We find a few poor schools with good principals, but we don't find any good schools with poor principals. (p. 28)*

The assumption, however, that a school principal could single-handedly provide the instructional leadership to propel an entire school toward educational excellence turned out to need further examination.

Two forces in education have increasingly factored into and enlarged what it means to take instructional leadership. In the twenty-plus years since instructional leadership first became synonymous with school leadership, computer technology and the standards movement have had far-reaching effects on public education. Increasingly sophisticated technology has made both aggregated and disaggregated student achievement data much more accessible, allowing educators to more easily assess the impact of curricular design and instructional practices on student achievement. And because the standards movement brings with it high expectations for *all* students, schools can apply their new data muscle in working to achieve more comprehensive effectiveness. Together, the goal of high expectations for all and the means to analyze effectiveness for all provide schools with the basis for improving. At the same time, leading this kind of effort is a bigger job than principals have ever faced.

In response, notions of shared governance, shared leadership, and, now, distributed leadership have come to the fore. Richard Elmore (2000) makes clear why distributed leadership is hard to get right, but also how vital such leadership is to the improvement of instructional practices:

> *Distributed leadership poses the challenge of how to distribute responsibility and authority for guidance and direction of instruction, and learning about instruction, so as to increase the likelihood that the decisions of individual teachers and principals about what to do, and what to learn how to do, aggregate into collective benefits for student learning. (p. 18)*

In 1991, in recognition of the complexity of instructional leadership, and incorporating internal and external evaluations of CSLA's ongoing effectiveness, we made a major shift in our approach to school leadership. In addition to focusing on the role of principals, we began a focus on the role of school leadership teams (SLTs). We have been refining that focus ever since.

For example, in designing the initial CSLA program for school teams, we drew on our experience, validated by a study about our work with principals (Marsh et al., 1990), to address the problem that although principals who went through the CSLA program learned and practiced many aspects of instructional leadership at their sites, they had a fragmented view of instructional leadership, seeing it in incremental rather than transformational terms. Many described their instructional leadership as episodic and event-based.

In response to these and related issues, the new program for school leadership teams was designed specifically so that school teams would be able to assess their schools' instructional improvement needs, determine appropriate site-level interventions, and evaluate the effectiveness of their interventions. The interventions were expected to involve comprehensive, schoolwide change — change that would substantially improve student achievement.

Although CSLA's program for school teams has focused from its inception on the improvement of student achievement, the twelve regional centers where the program was conducted lacked a unifying process that school teams could use. By 1998, the collective work of Mike Schmoker, Jim Cox, Richard Sagor, and Steven Thompson had emerged as a well-articulated continuous improvement planning process (see Lesson One) that CSLA adopted in all of our regional centers. We were at the point of having learned how to work well with school teams (in addition to individual administrators), we had a history of focusing in general on student achievement, and we now had a process that allowed for unrelenting attention to improved student learning. We had achieved a coherence of purpose and method that could support our vision of a well-functioning school leadership team.

What Is the CSLA Vision of a School Leadership Team?

CSLA recognizes that its definition of a school leadership team is distinctive. In many parts of the country a school leadership team is a body responsible for site-based decision-making. It is a school's shared-governance structure, and it addresses the wide range of issues involved in the daily operation of a school. This is not the role of school leadership teams that follow the CSLA model.

A school leadership team in the CSLA sense is a collection of people focused solely on supporting the improvement of student achievement at their school. The team is formed in numerous contextually appropriate ways and always includes the active participation of the principal, teacher leaders, classified staff, and a district liaison. Some teams include parents, community members, and students.

School leadership teams in the CSLA sense build the capacity of the school staff to participate in a continuous improvement planning process. The focus of this process is on student achievement and creating cultural norms in a school to support it. In many cases these school leadership teams see themselves as stewards and monitors of quality implementation of the instructional strategies and programs that have been selected to achieve a high-leverage student achievement improvement goal.

In our work with school leadership teams, we are guided by our latest mission statement and statement of results (see Appendix A), which themselves are informed by the California Professional Standards for Educational Leaders. (These standards and their descriptions of practice are found in *Moving Leadership Standards into Everyday Work: Descriptions of Practice,* WestEd, 2003.)

While much of the work of school leadership teams is done at their school sites, one of the roles of the CSLA School Leadership Team Development Program is to host seminars that bring teams together periodically to share their experiences and further explore the continuous improvement process (see Figure 1). School leadership teams attend ten to fifteen days of seminars over two or three years, and they are joined in these seminars by teams from four or more other schools. Back at their sites, teams engage in a similar number of local intersession days, planning and working with staff and keeping in touch with their district liaison.

Figure 1. School Leadership Team Development Program

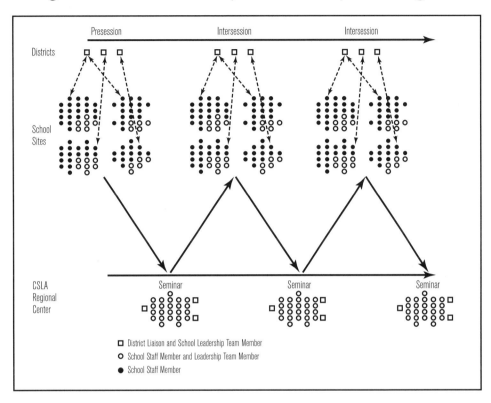

District Liaison and School Leadership Team Member

School Staff Member and Leadership Team Member

School Staff Member

What Lessons from School Leadership Teams Are Explored in This Book?

The nine lessons in this book are drawn from our experience with school leadership teams and from the schools themselves. They are supported and amplified by school improvement theory and research. Brief case histories demonstrate the lessons in action.

Lesson One, "Focus the Team's Work on the Continuous Improvement of Student Achievement," offers a model of continuous improvement planning and describes its major phases.

Lesson Two, "Create a Supportive School Culture through a Persistent Focus on Student Achievement," describes learning to consciously consider how the team plans to influence organizational culture.

Lesson Three, "Build Commitment and Focus before the Team Begins Its Work," points out how preliminary understandings about purpose, roles, and responsibilities can increase the likelihood of a school leadership team's success.

Lesson Four, "Pay Attention to Who's on the Team," enumerates the factors to consider in formulating team membership.

Lesson Five, "Use Real Work to Build the Team," highlights the effectiveness of shared, authentic work to build a cohesive, effective team.

Lesson Six, "Facilitate the Transition of the Team from Learners to Learners-as-Leaders," outlines the skills of leadership and describes the transition from teacher to teacher leader.

Lesson Seven, "Ensure Principal Commitment," points out the importance of principal commitment to the team and discusses the principal's role in creating "structural tension."

Lesson Eight, "Develop Teacher Leadership," describes the importance of teacher leadership and provides examples of teacher leadership actions.

Lesson Nine, "Align the Support of the District," describes ways district support can accelerate a school leadership team's work and, conversely, how unaligned district actions can scuttle months of a team's effort.

The Epilogue is a glimpse of new lessons that are evolving as CSLA continues its work with school leadership teams.

Finally, to illuminate the way CSLA works with schools and districts, appendices reproduce a number of CSLA tools and documents.

Focus the Work

The single most important event of the school year is the time we set aside for annual improvement planning. As goes planning, so goes the school's changes for improvement that year.

—Mike Schmoker
*The Results Fieldbook:
Practical Strategies from
Dramatically Improved
Schools*

LESSON ONE

Focus the Team's Work on the Continuous Improvement of Student Achievement — It's Doable

AT A GLANCE

Leadership teams learn to use a continuous improvement planning process (CIPP) to focus and guide the work of their school.

This lesson offers a model of continuous improvement planning and describes its major phases. Brief case histories clarify how the process has been used to improve student achievement.

An inner-city elementary school with 1,200 low-income and primarily Spanish-speaking students was served by a school leadership team that focused the staff's efforts on continuously improving levels of literacy among all of its students. Reading and other related scores began to rise. With a new principal, however, the team's focus fragmented, their capacity to lead declined, and student performance plateaued.

School leaders are surrounded by — in fact, inundated with — messages about the needs of their school. Not infrequently, the needs of students and staff are eclipsed by the more public issues of safety, accountability, and funding; by demands from the district; or even by a balky physical plant.

With so many needs competing for attention, it can be difficult for a school leadership team (SLT) to select and focus on any area as the centerpiece of their work. Yet as public education shifts to a standards-based system, opportunities to increase the focus of SLTs on student achievement have emerged. In 1996, Mike Schmoker's book, *Results: The Key to Continuous School Improvement,* offered a model of continuous improvement of student achievement, and CSLA embraced it.[1]

Phases of the Continuous Improvement Planning Process

Over the past several years, CSLA has implemented, evaluated, and refined the continuous improvement planning process (CIPP) that is at the heart of all our work with elementary, middle, and high school SLTs. We take all school leadership teams through the following phases of the continuous improvement planning process to help them develop the knowledge and skills necessary to lead continuous improvement at their sites (see also Figure 2):

- Readiness: Analyze the readiness of the school and its SLT to engage in continuous improvement of student achievement and the readiness of the school district to support their efforts.

- Taking stock: Review and analyze student achievement data, including all significant student subgroups.

- Goal setting: Based on analysis of student data, set student achievement improvement goals that meet the criteria for a well-written goal and ensure that each individual has no more than one goal to which he or she is responsible at any one time.

- Research and action plan: Conduct research that leads to the development of an action plan for implementing one or more strategies that will lead to achieving a goal.

---

[1] CSLA's continuous improvement planning process (CIPP) is adapted from the work of Mike Schmoker (1996, 1998a, 1998b), Jim Cox (1994), Richard Sagor (1993), and Steven R. Thompson (1997).

Figure 2. Major Phases of the CSLA Continuous Improvement Planning Process (CIPP)

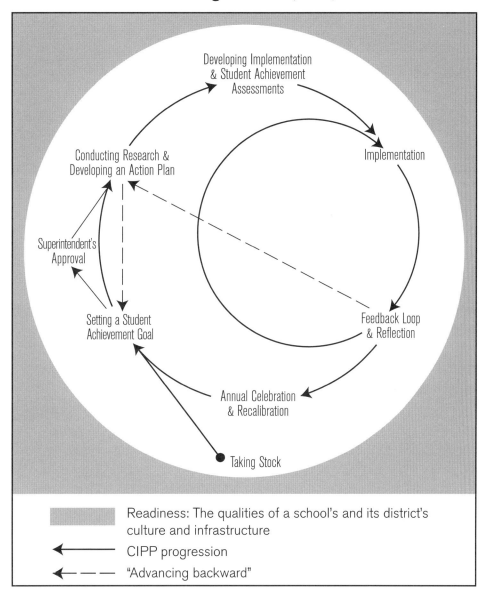

Developing Implementation & Student Achievement Assessments

Implementation

Conducting Research & Developing an Action Plan

Superintendent's Approval

Setting a Student Achievement Goal

Feedback Loop & Reflection

Annual Celebration & Recalibration

Taking Stock

Readiness: The qualities of a school's and its district's culture and infrastructure

CIPP progression

"Advancing backward"

- Developing assessments: Develop two assessment plans: (1) a plan for assessing the implementation of the selected strategies, and (2) a plan for assessing changes in student achievement as a result of the fully implemented strategies.

- Implementation: Put the action plan into play.

- Feedback loop and reflection: Develop a monthly data analysis and corrective action process for review of implementation progress and the impact of the plan on student achievement, and for adjustment of the strategies.

- Annual celebration and recalibration: Prepare an annual public report of summative results, both good and bad, with appropriate celebrations of progress toward the student achievement goals and preparations to enter the next cycle of improvement.

Readiness

Readiness represents the *culture* and *infrastructure* of the school (and its district) seeking to engage in continuous improvement. Some schools enter the process of continuous improvement with cultural norms and organizational values and capacities aligned with those required by the process; they are relatively "ready" to start. Other schools and districts may have historical patterns and relationships that interfere with participation in the process. These schools will have to unlearn old patterns, develop new practices, and forge new relationships in order to proceed. Schools develop the capacity to participate in continuous improvement at different rates, but typically those schools that are more ready make progress more quickly than those that are less ready.

Not all schools develop the capacity to continuously improve student achievement. Most often, an inability to progress is due to a nonalignment of school and district cultural norms with the norms necessary to engage in continuous improvement (see Lesson Two for a discussion of school culture). In addition, the infrastructure necessary to support the school and its team may be absent. Figure 3 provides examples of what can constitute lack of readiness.

It is easy for a fledgling group of teachers and their principal, who have yet to become a team with a shared purpose and mutual trust, to become discouraged and flounder when confronted with the task of reshaping norms that are inconsistent with continuous improvement or when the infrastructure they need to complete their work is absent. In some cases, the combination of cultural nonalignment and the lack of infrastructure is so debilitating that even the combined will of team members is insufficient for carrying out the work required.

Figure 3. When Readiness for CIPP Is Absent

CULTURAL NONALIGNMENT: EXAMPLES

Grade-level meetings: Complaining about school issues is the norm. Therefore, participants have little capacity to examine student work, make data-driven decisions, or learn from one another.

Use of time: The contract between the district and the teachers' association is written in such a way that SLT members are not permitted time to gather their colleagues together to focus on student achievement or associated instructional practices in any meaningful way.

Leadership: A school where teachers who assume leadership roles are maligned or treated suspiciously by colleagues may be incapable of developing the patterns of distributed leadership necessary to support continuous improvement.

LACK OF INFRASTRUCTURE: EXAMPLES

Assessments: An eighth-grade interdisciplinary team seeks to improve student writing, but the district has no districtwide writing assessment tools or practices to gauge the quality of student work.

Facilities: In a K-8 school, the only location where staff can meet is a large, drafty cafeteria, and seating is at cafeteria tables.

Capacity: An elementary school staff needs disaggregated data about the reading comprehension of its third-grade Hispanic boys. The district's technology services cannot provide the data or else cannot provide it when needed.

Taking Stock

Although a school can begin anywhere in the continuous improvement planning process, most begin by taking stock. Taking stock is an annual process of developing a shared understanding of the school's current reality related to student achievement and other selected factors. Data are at the heart of the taking stock phase.

When taking stock, a school community

- analyzes key indicators of student success — those related to the preceding year's student achievement improvement goals and other related factors;

- identifies points for celebration and celebrates publicly;

- identifies areas of student achievement that require continued attention and shares them publicly;

- makes all data public; and

- lays the groundwork for the establishment of a goal to guide improvement for the next year.

It is usually the case that data analysis skills must be taught to a school leadership team; the SLT, in turn, must become sufficiently knowledgeable to plan, organize, and facilitate the school staff's analysis of key indicators of student success and disaggregated data for subgroups of students. (For example, a school staff's ability to skillfully examine the data for low-performing high school students is critical to addressing unseen or ignored schoolwide or districtwide issues, and can begin to shift the perceived responsibility for all students' achievement to classroom practices and programs up and down the grades.)

In traditionally scheduled schools, taking stock occurs anywhere from late spring through early fall, depending on the availability of data. In year-round schools, taking stock may occur several times a year as groups of teachers "track on or off."

Goal Setting

Once student achievement data are analyzed, SLTs set achievement improvement goals. It is sensible to start with a single schoolwide goal. The rationale for this tight focus stems from years of experience of numerous experts in school reform and organizational development. As long ago as 1976, Peter Drucker was advising managers to limit their initiatives to those "where superior performance produces outstanding results." Michael Fullan (1991) warns of "massive failure" if schools attempt too many simultaneous initiatives. Robert Evans's (1996) advice about school change makes a similar point: "[E]ffective leaders target their energies, centering their time and effort on a short list of key issues, even if this means ignoring others." In his presentation at the 1998 CSLA convocation, Mike Schmoker repeated this advice and urged that no staff member work on more than one or at most two school or department goals during a given school year.

The complexities of continuous improvement require the development of new skills, a new infrastructure, new relationships, new information, and new processes. Schools will always be able to identify more than one worthy schoolwide goal, but as a school leadership team begins to learn the continuous improvement planning process, limiting the focus increases the chance for success. Our experience at CSLA has been with teams that focus on a single, high-leverage, schoolwide student achievement improvement goal. When they do, the targeted student achievement increases. Once a school has developed the skills, infrastructure, relationships, information, and processes required, school members might consider the adoption of a second schoolwide student achievement improvement goal or several goals each specific to smaller units within the school (i.e., grade-level teams or departments). The key is that no member of the staff have more than one improvement goal to focus on at any given time.

A student achievement improvement goal is most effective when it is set by those responsible for its attainment. It is not the role of the school leadership team to establish the goal for an interdisciplinary team, a department, a grade level, or the staff. Instead, the role of the school leadership team is to build the capacity of these groups to set a goal that addresses a high-leverage problem that has been identified through a shared analysis of the relevant data. A goal set by a school leadership team is likely to have the same acceptance as a goal imposed by the principal, the district, or the state working in isolation from those responsible for its achievement. This does not mean, however, that a school leadership team cannot propose a variety of goals in order to model a format or initiate a discussion among the school staff.

Effective goals are SMART goals. The goal is *specific* and therefore written in clear, simple language. The goal is *measurable* because it targets student achievement that can be quantified and, when necessary, uses multiple measures. The goal is realistic and therefore *attainable*. The goal is *relevant* because it is supported by a clear rationale and has been approved by the superintendent or his or her designee. A *time frame* for the achievement of the goal is clearly stated, making the goal time bound. (See Figure 4 for examples of SMART goals.)

Figure 4. What Does a SMART Goal Look Like?

A SMART goal is Specific, Measurable, Attainable, Relevant, and Time bound. Two examples below demonstrate student achievement improvement goals that meet these criteria:

1. On the May writing assessment, 85 percent of the students will move upward two or more levels on the writing rubric. The remaining 15 percent will show improvement. Students with an initial score of 5 [the next-to-highest level on the writing rubric] will maintain that score or move upward one level; students with an initial score of 6 will maintain that score.

2. The Middletown Elementary School staff have decided to place our primary focus during the next three years on promoting student literacy. Our decision is based on the following factors:

   - the need for all students to meet district and state content standards in language arts, and

   - the superintendent's goal for all students to become fluent readers by the end of third grade.

   Schoolwide, 64 percent of our students are currently meeting grade-level standards in language arts.

   The goal for the primary grades (K-3) is that by 2002, 80 percent of the students completing third grade at Middletown Elementary School will be fluent readers. Student performance will be assessed with the following measures: running records (grades K-2); report cards and SAT 9 reading scores (grades 2-3). The students in the Resource Specialist Program will demonstrate accelerated growth in reading (six to seven levels on the running record).

   The goal for the elementary grades (4-6) is for 80 percent of the students completing sixth grade at Middletown Elementary School to be competent readers. Student performance will be assessed with the following measures: report cards (C or better) and SAT 9 reading scores (50th percentile or greater). The students in the Resource Specialist Program will demonstrate accelerated growth in reading (1.5 years or more).

Superintendent's Approval

In most cases a school will submit student achievement goals to the superintendent for approval, ensuring that district policies and resources will support their efforts. (See Lesson Nine for a discussion of aligning school goals with district support.)

Research and Action Plan

Once a student achievement improvement goal has been adopted, those responsible for its attainment investigate the current practices in the school related to achieving the goal. Additional research may focus on strategies (programs) that are successful in similar schools, as well as initiatives discussed in education journals, at education workshops, and at education conferences.

In some cases, a strategy is determined by the district staff, who require all schools to implement it. More frequently, however, those responsible for achieving the school goal select the strategy that they believe will work best with their students.

Once a strategy has been selected, an action plan, composed of action steps, is developed. The action steps are placed on a timeline, and those individuals responsible for completing each action step are identified. The individual or team responsible for monitoring the action plan is named.

A strategy is viewed as a hypothesis. A school that practices the continuous improvement planning process considers each strategy for implementing the student achievement improvement goal to be a well-researched hypothesis, nothing more. The school seeks proof of the effectiveness of a strategy.

Developing Assessments

A school leadership team must develop a means of testing its hypothesis. Testing involves the collection of two sets of data: (1) data related to the degree of implementation of the strategy, and (2) data related to the targeted student achievement improvement goal.

In *Building Implementation Capacity for Continuous Improvement,* Kristin Donaldson Geiser, et al. discuss the cycle of evaluation:

> *We have found it to be helpful...to conceptualize the cycle of evaluation as two interrelated cycles: evaluation of implementation and evaluation of impact. The first cycle focuses on the actual process of implementation:*

in order to implement a particular strategy effectively, schools must always be in the process of assessing the degree to which they have sufficiently addressed each of the elements of implementation with regard to that strategy.

The second cycle includes ongoing reflection regarding the impact on student learning of the strategy being implemented. As schools develop the ability to engage in both of these cycles simultaneously, they are engaging in the dynamic process of implementation. When they are not attending to either cycle in a continuous way, they face many challenges. (p. 7)

A powerful strategy that is poorly implemented can produce poor results. If both implementation data and student results data associated with a strategy are not obtained, then a successful strategy could be eliminated — or an ineffective one could be retained. If the degree of implementation of a given strategy is not understood, then decisions regarding eliminating or allocating resources to a "best" strategy will remain haphazard, a matter of opinion.

Most school leadership teams, schools, and districts are relatively unsophisticated when it comes to monitoring the implementation of their strategies. CSLA has found, for example, that SLTs struggle to set criteria that describe a strategy or program that is ideally implemented. Teams' response to this challenge is often shocked silence. Most educators have not been trained to detail what must be accomplished and to be able to say with confidence that a chosen strategy has been fully implemented in their school. The concept of criteria is not well-understood. Furthermore, there is little evidence that those responsible for seeing that a strategy is well-implemented have the capacity to collect data related to such criteria.

The solution is to teach SLTs to develop implementation criteria and the means of measuring the progress of implementation, but also to expect them to need some time to become accomplished at monitoring implementation. CSLA asks teams to monitor implementation frequently throughout a year so that they can make adjustments not foreseen in the original action planning process.

A second plan for data collection focuses on the student achievement that is an intended result of the strategy. CSLA asks school leadership teams to select measures of student achievement that can provide information on a thirty-day cycle to those who are implementing the strategy.

A strategy that is only partially implemented cannot be expected to produce the same level of student achievement improvement as one that is fully implemented. Thus, all student achievement improvement data gathered prior to full implementation of a strategy provide an incomplete picture of its impact, although its possible impact may be projected. Once the data indicate that the criteria for full implementation have been met, the student achievement data become a powerful way to determine if the selected strategy is having the envisioned impact.

If the data are positive, then the strategy can be placed on a periodic review status while more attention is focused on additional strategies. If the student achievement data indicate a less-than-satisfactory impact, those responsible for the strategy's implementation might fine-tune the strategy for a given amount of time or else eliminate it in order to free up resources for new strategies.

Implementation

"Schooling" is the common term that describes the implementation aspect of the continuous improvement planning process. Teachers engage students in curriculum and instruction designed to facilitate learning — for all students. They implement strategies along with the daily adjustments required by the ever-changing context of a school and its people. Some days are magical; others are less wondrous. Unforeseen challenges continually arise, for new and veteran teachers alike. It is the teacher's minute-by-minute decisions that make a difference in student learning and achievement.

These implementation lessons are captured, made explicit, and shared among colleagues in monthly data analysis and corrective action meetings, which occur in the feedback loop and reflection phase.

Feedback Loop and Reflection

At the heart of continuous improvement are many small meetings. Informed by strategy implementation data and the accompanying student achievement impact data, small groups of teachers (grade-level teams, primary teams, intermediate teams, interdisciplinary teams, content teams, departments) meet monthly to determine what they have learned and what further steps need to be taken. In these meetings, teachers can openly discuss their day-to-day efforts to help students meet very specific achievement goals and whether these efforts have resulted in student improvement.

They can identify professional development needs, organize support for each other, give and receive coaching support, and freely share materials and methods. These collaborative meetings are the authentic work of teachers focused on improving their classroom practice.

All phases of the continuous improvement planning process provide key information that focuses, supports, and gives direction and purpose to the meetings. Just as the teacher-student interaction is the most important component of student success, the data analysis and corrective action meeting is the most important component of teacher success.

To help school leadership teams support their teachers, CSLA teaches SLTs to

- design the data analysis and corrective action meetings, and
- facilitate these meetings.

CSLA also works with principals and district leaders to provide

- time for data analysis and corrective action meetings,
- information necessary for the meetings, and
- appropriate environments for the meetings.

Teams come to realize several benefits when small groups of teachers regularly focus on the continuous improvement of their classroom practice and work to implement a student achievement improvement goal. Teams report

- more frequent feedback to teachers about strategy implementation and student impact,
- higher levels of collaboration among teachers,
- more teacher involvement, and
- deeper dialogue about teaching and learning.

Annual Celebration and Recalibration

The completion of a cycle is significant. All schools, even those with complex, year-round schedules, have rhythmic cycles with a definite beginning and a definite end. These powerfully symbolic moments in time are also an important aspect of any continuous improvement planning process. It is essential that the SLT and, ultimately, the entire school staff experience the complete continuous improvement planning process cycle at least once a year. The closure of a cycle is critical to the opening of the next cycle.

In continuous improvement schools, some forms of data are available throughout the year. Teachers use these formative data in their corrective action meetings to analyze student progress and understand the impact of their efforts. Summative data, however, from either districtwide tests or state-mandated, norm-referenced tests, may not be available until after the close of school or after the opening of the next term. This makes for a data cycle that is out of sync with the student calendar. School leadership teams that understand the power of ritual do not permit this circumstance to deter them from the opportunity to celebrate and recalibrate.

In the fall or whenever summative data are available, and armed with data regarding the progress made toward meeting the student achievement improvement goal, the team facilitates the staff's final analysis. (See Figure 5 for examples of data.) The SLT asks various groups of teachers to identify areas for celebration and areas for renewed attention, focusing especially on the areas related to the school's student achievement improvement goals. The whole staff then explores and discusses the results, and the school leadership team facilitates the development of a consensus about areas of celebration and of renewed focus. The SLT also sets a time for a public celebration and prepares a report about agreed-upon recalibrations for the future.

The celebration of student results is a carefully planned event and a highlight of the year. Students and the school community are invited, and students, parents, teachers, other school staff, and school leaders are recognized for their contribution to the school's success. Also, the recalibrated student achievement improvement goals are announced and community members are asked for specific support.

CSLA has found that it is a challenge for school leadership teams to design these celebrations. Schools typically celebrate student growth with ceremonies for students — those who have been on the honor roll, won citizenship awards, won attendance awards, and so on. But the staff who deserve credit for data-verified improvement of student achievement seem to feel that public recognition of their work is not appropriate. Teams may be hesitant to organize such events. Since these celebrations are an important part of the continuous improvement cycle, until they become routine, a reminder from an outside facilitator or a school coach may be required.

Figure 5. Celebration and Recalibration Data

Plans for assessing student achievement call for the following data to be available to the school leadership teams in the celebration and recalibration phase of CIPP:

- demographic data
- student and teacher attendance data
- student discipline data
- achievement data
  - course
  - teacher/interdisciplinary team
  - grade-level
  - department
  - whole-school
  - district
  - state
  - disaggregated/subgroup
  - matched longitudinal/multiyear

School leadership teams often feel more at ease identifying areas for renewed focus, since identifying areas of deficit is part of a school's traditional review process. But because any review has the potential to expose a large number of needs, SLTs must help their staffs resist developing several new goals to meet these needs. As we emphasized earlier, choosing too many goals dilutes focus, scatters resources, and minimizes impact. Furthermore, a significant part of a new beginning is developing a clear focus; in the case of a new student improvement cycle, that would mean identifying only one or two student achievement goals.

SLTs have found that because schools are *systems*, even though a team begins with a focus on the continuous improvement of student achievement, the other parts of the system improve as an indirect result of the team's steady focus on what matters most. (See Lesson Two for the effect on school culture, for example, when the whole staff focuses on one or two student achievement goals.)

Three Supporting Conditions

A focus on the continuous improvement of student achievement requires that three conditions be anticipated and prepared for. First, it goes without saying that SLTs need access to data, but providing it is rarely simple. Second, any goal a school staff sets will only be as powerful as the degree to which each staff member personally embraces it and understands where the school is in relation to it; thus, "structural tension" must be made personal. Finally, schools must be prepared to "advance backward," and to recognize that the continuous improvement process will sometimes cause them to back up before moving on.

Provide Access to Data

In order to engage in continuous improvement of student achievement, the school must have access to data (not to mention the time, cultural capacity, and skill to analyze it). Demographic data, attendance data, and disciplinary data, as well as student achievement data, are needed. Data for multiple years must be available for the whole school, for grades, for content areas, for teachers, and for subgroups of students. Customized data must be available monthly to small groups of teachers (e.g., grade-level teams, teachers teaching common courses, departments, interdisciplinary teams). The demand for data will challenge the technological capacity of the school and the district to provide it.

Make Structural Tension Personal

Robert Fritz, in *The Path of Least Resistance for Managers: Designing Organizations to Succeed*, states that the "principle of structural tension — knowing what we want to create and knowing where we are in relationship to our goals — is the most powerful force an organization can have."

Ideally, structural tension resides within each individual in an organization. If the principal of the school feels the tension between a school's reality and its goal, or even if the SLT feels the tension, this does not mean that the staff of the school are experiencing the same degree of structural tension. In order for the school leadership to use the power of the structural tension model, the leaders must provide the opportunity for each member of the staff and the school community to develop a deeply held sense of current reality. In addition, the staff must be intimately involved in setting the goal that they wish to achieve. The degree to which each staff member is involved in the process, making the tension his or her own, is the degree to which he or she will be motivated to close the gap between current reality and the goal.

Thus, organizational progress occurs when the staff makes deep sense of their school's data. The staff must be given the skills, time, and facilitation to understand the current reality of their school. An analysis of data passed down from the district, with little opportunity for the school staff to develop understanding of it, is relatively ineffective. The staff must also understand the data well enough to set an improvement goal, since in the end they are responsible for achieving it. At both ends of the structural tension model, those responsible for bringing improvement to the system must "own the tension."

Structural tension is embedded in the continuous improvement planning process. It is created by completion of the taking stock and goal planning phases. Structural tension is also created in the process of action planning. When criteria are established to define a fully implemented strategy, tension is the result. Each data analysis and corrective action meeting is an example of defining current reality and refining strategies to improve that reality. The role of the SLT is to create shared tension among the members of the school staff. The team then facilitates the collaboration of all the staff to resolve this tension. The CIPP helps to facilitate both the creation of structural tension and its resolution. (See Lesson Seven for a discussion of the principal's role with regard to structural tension.)

Be Prepared to "Advance Backward"

At first glance, the continuous improvement planning process might appear to be a simple progression: Begin by taking stock, proceed to goal planning, move on to goal writing, and so on. But given the wide range of readiness exhibited by schools and their districts, the implementation of this process is much less sequential. An SLT or a school may complete one phase and move on to the next, only to discover that the level of understanding or support gained in the previous phase is inadequate for completion of the current phase. So the SLT or school "advances backward" to the previous phase and completes it with a renewed appreciation of its complexity. Data analysis and corrective action meetings are designed to influence and modify the action plan, necessitating a return to the goal planning phase. Skilled teams anticipate ambiguity and the need to revisit phases; they benefit from learning along the way. They are not fooled into thinking that continuous improvement is as simple as taking one phase at a time.

A Case in Point: Riverside Unified School District

When nineteen schools in the Riverside Unified School District were identified by the state as underperforming, Susan Rainey, the district's superintendent, was puzzled by the contrast between high-performing schools and those that were struggling.

The district had been implementing the highly regarded results-based instruction outlined by Mike Schmoker in *Results: The Key to Continuous School Improvement.* Schmoker encourages teachers to continuously assess students throughout the academic year and adjust curricula based on student results. Although the principals of every Riverside school were committed to Schmoker's model, Rainey found that when she surveyed classrooms throughout the district, many teachers were not practicing results-based instruction. Some teachers had resisted Schmoker's ideas, but many simply didn't understand how to apply them in their classrooms. At that point, Rainey decided to form school leadership teams. "It shouldn't be just the principal who is the purveyor of knowledge," Rainey says. "Results had to become a part of the school culture."

The CSLA project director in the Riverside County Office of Education, Richard Martinez, met with Rainey and her cabinet members to design the two-year Results Renaissance Program (RRP), which would involve teachers as well as principals in three to five annual training sessions based on Schmoker's book.

"It's like the roots of a tree," Martinez says. "In the first year of the results program, the root structure is not deep. What Sue and her district were looking for was a process to do some very deep watering to get those roots to grow into a very deep level of the culture."

The RRP aimed to ensure that every teacher in the district bought into the importance of testing and results-based curricula and knew what it meant for their classroom practice.

Together with CSLA, Rainey and her cabinet members selected five schools for the initial phase of the program. Two of the schools accelerated so quickly during the first year that they moved out of the program and were replaced by two new schools. By June of the first year, the district's average Academic Performance Index (API) had risen significantly. Bill Ermert, the assistant superintendent for educational alternatives and services, credits CSLA's School Leadership Team Development Program for the district's success. "The leadership teams are the most critical thing, in my opinion, because if you don't have the teacher buy-in, they're not going to contribute ideas to the strategy sessions or enthusiastically share their knowledge," he said. "You can't ever enact real change without that."

During the first year, about 40 teachers, representing each grade level and subject at the five schools, gathered for three day-long training sessions with the principals, the nine cabinet members, and the superintendent. In the first training session, the group learned to apply Schmoker's model: test students, analyze the data and develop instructional strategies to address problems, and work with an assigned cabinet member to brainstorm solutions to current problems and create goals for the upcoming months until the next RRP session. During the second year, schools created on-campus school leadership teams that mirrored the work of the RRP teams.

Lorie Reitz, the principal of Ramona High School, found the sessions to be a powerful catalyst for creating successful instructional strategy. When teachers on Ramona's English Academic Impact Leadership Team asserted that they shouldn't be solely responsible for solving the school's literacy problem, Reitz integrated English language arts strategies into every academic department. "It's not only the English teachers' responsibility to teach the standards," Reitz says. "Now it's everybody's responsibility."

The joint effort paid off quickly in Ramona's social studies department. In just three months, students improved their scores on a weekly QuickWrite assessment by a range of 15 to 21 percent. In April, the school's Social Studies Academic Impact Leadership Team set a goal to improve student writing mechanics to 80 percent accuracy in sentence structure, grammar, and punctuation. By June, two of the four classes met the goal, one class improved from 20 to 40 percent accuracy, and one class improved from 7 to 28 percent accuracy.

Today, only two schools in the Riverside Unified School District are in danger of being labeled underperforming, but Rainey isn't about to relax: "I am so convinced this is a good direction for us to go that I'm asking each school in the district to go through a two-year School Leadership Team Development Program with CSLA, regardless of what the scores are. I guess I'm a convert because I see the impact of leadership teams when they are an integral part of instruction decisions."

(See the rubric developed in the Riverside district to monitor schools' implementation of the CIPP, "Results-Meeting Rubric: Implementation Stages," Appendix B.)

LESSON TWO

Create a Supportive School Culture through a Persistent Focus on Student Achievement — It's a Double Win

AT A GLANCE

A school leadership team can change the culture of its school by engaging the school staff in a continuous improvement planning process.

This lesson describes how teams can plan to influence organizational culture. Case histories provide examples of SLTs' impact on culture.

The school leadership team of a middle school struggled to address two issues: (1) the dysfunctional school culture and (2) student achievement. The results were strikingly mixed. When the team focused their attention and team development on student achievement, their teamwork and impact were superb. But when they worked directly on the school's dysfunctional culture, they unraveled as a team. The team disbanded after two years and recommended that a new team form, with the single focus of improving student achievement. This recommendation was carried out and two years later the school became a California Distinguished School, meeting the criteria set by California's standards-based review; achievement scores rose; and the relationships among the school's adults improved.

The previous brief history might suggest that if a school engages in a continuous improvement process, it will never need to attend to school culture — that improved school culture is a by-product of the process. And it is. But it is also true that as school leadership teams become more sophisticated, they learn a number of strategies that accelerate the improvement of school culture rather than simply enable it.

Intervening in School Culture

Organizations, like individuals, have identities. As with personal identities, organizational identities are built upon experiences, beliefs, and values. In a school organization, identity is the product of the shared experiences, beliefs, and values of its staff, students, and community. For example, a school with a history of successful students might have an organizational identity of itself as efficacious; it might have beliefs and values that, as a school, it can and should meet the needs of just about any student. A less successful school might question its own ability to teach successfully and might be prone to make excuses for the lack of success.

When school leadership teams think about affecting school culture, it is the school's "deep" structures — beliefs, values, and identity — that they have in mind (see Figure 6). Deep structures not only define an organization, they are crucial to maintaining its stability. This fact can create a challenge.

In some organizations, the deep structures are a straitjacket. The organization is immobilized by its own structures: It is unable to adapt. Yet schools taking on the continuous improvement process must adapt — to the new organizational patterns that the process requires. The challenge to leaders, then, is to influence the deep structures of the organization in order to permit behavior consistent with continuous improvement.

At the surface level, leaders can change the environment by cleaning, painting, moving furniture, and so on. Additionally, leaders can consider the environment of the organization's meetings. Room arrangement, amenities, pacing or quality of facilitators, materials, planning for discussion and dialogue, and clear meeting outcomes are all examples of environmental conditions. Taken individually, each intervention may seem inconsequential. Collectively, however, when consistently applied, they create a significant impact.

Most professional development, however, is designed to intervene at the level of activities and behaviors that can lead to new skills. In this way, in time, new competencies can be built.

Figure 6. Organizational Levels of Intervention in School Culture

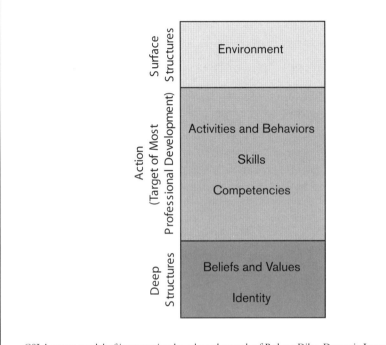

CSLA uses a model of intervention based on the work of Robert Dilts, Dynamic Learning Center, Santa Cruz, Calif., and Suzanne Bailey, Bailey Alliance, Vacaville, Calif.

At the deep level, however, the beliefs and values of an organization determine whether the organization will actually use the new skills. If interventions run counter to existing beliefs and values, they may be minimized or rejected. Beliefs and values are often beyond the reach of typical professional development interventions. Rational approaches alone may be unsuccessful in changing strong beliefs and values. CSLA incorporates Suzanne Bailey's (2000) "more-than-rational" change strategies in our recommendations for intervening at the deep level:

> *More-than-rational change strategies can be integrated to allow a different pace and depth to the change process. The use of dialogue, storytelling, metaphor, ritual, dramatization and ceremony add the capacity to pace strong feelings and deeply held attachments and lead to letting go and some excitement about new possibilities. (p. 9)*

A Case in Point: Joseph Gambetta Middle School

Members of the Joseph Gambetta Middle School SLT were learning the protocol for looking at student work, and they became caught up in a typical middle school conversation: "If the third-grade teachers would just teach the kids their multiplication facts, then we wouldn't be having so many problems teaching math!"

At that point, team members were prodded into examining just how many students still needed to learn their math facts. They realized that they didn't know. The team found out through a "quick and dirty" assessment that only 23 percent of the students knew their multiplication facts through the twelves tables with automaticity.

Team members decided to take one school day and organize the entire school support system (e.g., teachers, aides, parents) to ensure that all students knew their multiplication facts by the end of that day. Team members, with one exception, thought that this was a good idea. The exception was the math teacher on the team, who said that the idea was unworkable, but that he'd go along with the team's decision.

The team designed a "multiplication day." During each of the day's six periods, students moved to different multiplication-table learning activities. At the end of each period, they completed a quick assessment. Once a student met the goal of knowing the multiplication tables through the twelves with automaticity, he or she was put into reinforcement activities and given a pass to a preferred activity.

At the next CSLA seminar, team members could barely stay in their chairs when it was time for the SLTs to share their recent efforts. The reluctant math teacher jumped to his feet and proclaimed, "Before we tell you what we did, I need to tell you that our multiplication day was the best day of teaching that I've had in thirty-five years!" The team went on to report that for the first time in its history, their school had accomplished something together that was focused on student achievement. Team members said that they finally understood what was meant by a community of practice. And they were proud to report that 86 percent of their students now knew their multiplication tables with automaticity. They added that they were determined to get the remaining 14 percent up to par. They finished by stating that they couldn't wait to do more learning activities like this one — and that looking at student work on a regular basis would keep them informed about what to take on next.

As we said earlier, not all school leadership teams actively engage a school's culture. Especially when school leadership teams are first feeling their way, they may be satisfied to enjoy the incidental cultural benefits that derive from a schoolwide focus on student achievement. But a skilled school leadership team can focus a school's attention on improving student achievement while simultaneously changing the organizational environment. For such SLTs, a basic consideration is at which level of intervention to engage.

It almost goes without saying that if an SLT can improve environmental factors, they should. What meeting doesn't benefit from clear expected outcomes, a clean space, or refreshments, for example?

On the other hand, when considering whether to intervene at the general levels of action or belief, the choices are more complex. Intervening at either level, the goal is the same — to free the school from norms that are causing rigid behavior and to increase the organization's adaptive range of behaviors. Yet for one school leadership team it might be more appropriate to get at beliefs and values indirectly, while another might be comfortable with a more direct approach.

With an indirect approach, the leadership team would create organizational patterns that require different behaviors of individuals and that reveal past beliefs and values with regard to education practice that are no longer valid, presumably causing individuals to update their beliefs and values.

With a direct approach to beliefs and values, the leadership team might engage staff in a rational path of collegial sharing, revealing, testing, re-evaluating, and presumably altering their beliefs and values with regard to education practice. Alternatively, the SLT might employ more-than-rational approaches such as ritual, ceremony, metaphor, and dialogue to explore staff beliefs, values, and identity.

An SLT with extensive experience plans each professional development session with the intention of intervening at as many levels as possible and during each phase of the continuous improvement planning process. See the following descriptions of phase-by-phase interventions.

Addressing Culture While Taking Stock

As a school leadership team prepares to involve the staff to take stock, the team can plan on multiple levels. Taking stock can be viewed simply as data analysis that aims to answer the question, How are our students doing and what do we do next? A team that wishes to get even more out of the taking stock phase has many options, related to Robert Dilts's levels of intervention, from the surface structures of the environment through the deep structures of beliefs, values, and identity.

Environment

A high-performing team considers environmental conditions. A team might ask questions such as these as it plans a taking stock meeting:

- Do we organize people into small groups?
- Do we have the group work as a whole?
- Where should we have this meeting?
- How do we arrange the room, tables, and so on?
- What amenities — such as food, drink, music, or decorations — should we provide?
- Should we use a metaphor to describe the purpose of the event and its outcomes?
- How can we use graphics and other modes to represent information and data?
- How can we involve the district?
- What will be the opening and closing rituals?
- What materials and supplies are needed? How will they be organized?
- Should we use multimedia?
- Should we use graphic recording?
- How should we facilitate the meeting?
- How should we allocate time?
- How can we use the symbolic power of celebration?

Careful attention to environmental conditions can support learning, increase participants' receptivity, and create conditions in which deeper levels of dialogue are possible.

Activities and behaviors, skills, and competencies

An experienced SLT develops the activities and behaviors, skills, and competencies of staff colleagues. The SLT determines which activities and behaviors, skills, and competencies are required to complete the taking stock phase and plans to build them as needed. These might include the following:

- data collection practices
- data analysis skills

- multiple sources of data (triangulation)
- meeting design
- histomapping (a graphic representation of the school's history)
- context mapping (a graphic representation of the school's current context related to an issue)
- group process skills
- dialogue and discussion
- facilitation skills
- recording skills
- needs assessment
- timekeeping

Once staff members have mastered the necessary activities and behaviors, skills, and competencies, they can better focus their attention on the purpose of taking stock.

Beliefs

An expert SLT considers the beliefs it is trying to shape through the work. The taking stock phase has the potential to develop beliefs such as the following:
- Data help to increase our objectivity.
- Those students who do not meet the standards today can learn to meet the standards.
- Working together, we can make a difference for our students.

Values

Through the taking stock phase, a number of organizational features or values can emerge:
- celebration and persistence
- data-driven decision-making
- openness, honesty, and inclusiveness
- collaboration, interdependence, and proficiency
- flexibility and improvement
- increased diversity and accountability

Identity

Finally, a team has an impact on the school's identity by creating internal dialogue among staff members during the taking stock phase. Examples include the following:
- We are learners.
- Each of us is a significant member of this team.
- Each of us contributes to the achievement of our goal.

Addressing Culture during Goal Setting

Environment

During the goal setting phase, an SLT might focus on these environmental conditions:

- ground rules
- decision-making agreements
- alignment of the goal with district priorities

Activities and behaviors, skills, and competencies

Activities and behaviors, skills, and competencies that an SLT might choose to develop as part of the goal setting phase include the following:

- prioritization
- advocacy
- dialogue
- debate
- consensus

Beliefs

An SLT might try to develop beliefs such as these during the goal setting phase:

- Working toward a common goal, we can make it happen.
- We can select high-leverage goals.
- We are capable.

Values

Values that might emerge during a carefully planned goal setting phase include the following:

- shared focus
- efficacy
- coherence
- personal and group commitment
- motivation

Identity

A skillful school leadership team will help its staff develop an identity that includes the following:

- We are goal oriented.
- We make a difference.

Addressing Culture during Research and Action Planning

Environment

Environmental conditions that the SLT might create to support the research and action plan phase of the CIPP are as follows:

- access to expertise
- access to professional development
- access to literature
- district research support
- visitation access to other schools and districts

Activities and behaviors, skills, and competencies

The research and action plan phase might encourage the SLT to promote the following activities and behaviors, skills, and competencies for colleagues:

- brainstorming
- exploratory research into curriculum, instruction, and assessment practices
- program profiles
- action planning
- reflection
- filters for program selection

Beliefs

Beliefs that might result while the SLT guides the school through the phase of researching strategies and writing a hypothesis and action plan include the following:

- Our ongoing learning is vital.
- We must stay informed.
- We can select strategies that will achieve our goal.

Values

Several organizational values are likely to result from the process of hypothesis formation:

- professional development
- inquiry
- flexibility
- reflection

Identity

As a result of working together to research and develop an action plan, staff are likely to see themselves in these ways:

- We are developers of a living action plan.
- We are thoughtful, informed educators.

Addressing Culture While Developing Assessments

Environment

The SLT might plan to address these environmental factors during the assessment development phase:

- follow-through support from leadership
- access to expertise
- availability of district expertise
- support from another SLT
- facilitation

Activities and behaviors, skills, and competencies

Activities and behaviors, skills, and competencies that would be useful for the SLT to help staff build as they develop assessments include the following:

- developing criteria
- decision-making
- developing assessments
- monitoring timelines

Beliefs

An SLT might find that staff develop beliefs such as these through the assessment development process:

- We can implement valued strategies and programs at a high level.
- We can determine the impact of our actions.
- We can always improve what we do.

Values

The following values are likely to emerge from the development of implementation and impact assessments:

- effectiveness
- quality implementation
- human development
- organizational support
- student results

Identity

Schools that succeed in developing implementation and impact assessments also develop a related identity:

- We are proficient at our craft.
- We stand for quality.

Addressing Culture during Feedback and Reflection

Environment

The data analysis and corrective action meetings that constitute the feedback loop and reflection phase are the focus of the entire continuous improvement planning process. The SLT makes certain that the learning environment of these meetings is conducive to quality work. No detail is left to chance. Leaders at all levels attend to aspects of the environment, such as the following:

- allocation and use of time
- facilitation
- room arrangements
- availability and presentation of data
- amenities, such as food and drink
- graphics and decor
- follow-through support

Activities and behaviors, skills, and competencies

The SLT consciously develops the activities and behaviors, skills, and competencies necessary to support the effective work of their colleagues in the data analysis and corrective action meetings. An SLT might attend to the following, for example:

- facilitation skills
- brainstorming skills
- prioritization skills
- group process behaviors
- data analysis competency
- reflection on action
- Mike Schmoker's 30/30 meeting routines

Beliefs

Staff participation in these carefully planned meetings allows SLT members to help staff develop these beliefs:

- We can support and learn from one another.
- Collectively, we know a lot and can share our expertise.
- We can adjust our instruction throughout the year based on data.

Values

School staff can be expected to develop the following values as a result of the feedback and reflection phase — the corrective action meetings:

- collaboration
- teamwork
- shared commitment
- continuous improvement of students, self, and organization
- authentic work of embedded professional development
- flexibility and efficacy

Identity

By participating in the cycle of the continuous improvement process, school staff can be expected to develop an extremely positive organizational identity:

- We always improve.
- We are collaborators.
- We assist one another.
- We are open to new ways of doing things.

It is possible for a school leadership team to guide its school through the phases of the continuous improvement planning process at a relatively simple level: Each task is accomplished and the appropriate products from each phase (such as a goal statement or an action plan) are completed. A team that accomplishes this level of work is to be greatly commended for achieving significant growth. And much more is possible. As a team develops and gains understanding and experience, new possibilities open up. Thus, it is not unusual for a school to participate in the SLT program for five or more years, never completing the work that seems to continually reveal itself.

A Case in Point: Webster Elementary School

For more than thirteen years as a teacher at Webster Elementary School, Estella Coronado felt that she was letting her students down. Year after year, first graders in English Language Development (ELD), an English immersion program, entered her classroom reading below grade level. Despite her best efforts, they showed little improvement, remaining dependent on their native language, Spanish or Hmong.

Coronado was not alone in her frustration. Very few of Webster's students met grade-level reading standards until the school joined forces with the California School Leadership Academy (CSLA).

Then it happened. For the first time, one of Coronado's students learned to read at grade level. Coronado was ecstatic, but nothing prepared her for the following year's progress. Twelve of her twenty ELD students developed grade-level reading skills. Their success, Coronado says, is no mystery. It is the direct result of CSLA's contributions, which have spurred academic achievement throughout the campus and boosted the school's Academic Performance Index by a remarkable 105 points.

Schoolwide, when CSLA began coaching Webster's staff and administrators, only 28 percent of the school's 532 students were reading at grade level. According to Macmillan/McGraw-Hill test scores, 72 percent were reading below grade level. A year later, 32 percent of the student body was reading at grade level. Five months later, the school's literacy rate rose to 39 percent. Although still below state standards, Coronado is confident that the school's literacy rate will continue to rise.

CSLA's strategy at Webster is based on three fundamental principles: (1) team leadership, (2) test assessment, and (3) school culture. Traditionally, teachers are isolated, rarely sharing academic concerns across grade levels or developing standard solutions. CSLA emphasizes schoolwide communication, bringing teachers together for monthly forums and test assessment meetings, where they share ideas across grade levels and develop strategies to address poor test results. CSLA also organizes school leadership teams, which meet with school and district administrators to voice teacher concerns about what needs to be done and the support needed to do it.

At first, Coronado feared using monthly test assessments because they held her accountable for student progress, which, for more than a decade, had remained at a standstill. But during the past two years, as she and other teachers have used test results to restructure curricula to meet student needs, she has felt a sense of empowerment, caused by the rising test scores. It didn't take long before the whole school was working together, and student achievement skyrocketed.

"Every time I test the students, we graph the results together as a class," Coronado says. "I point out how much each person is growing and everybody cheers. I say, 'Let's do the happy dance!' and the kids love it."

Classroom celebration, a key component of the CSLA strategy, is reinforced by the spirit displayed campuswide on Tuesdays, when all teachers wear green shirts that read "Committed to Excellence." Some students have begun to mimic teacher enthusiasm by wearing their own green clothes to school on Tuesdays.

"It's a one-for-all, all-for-one mentality," Coronado says. "It's a big high. We've all bought into the idea that we can achieve great reading scores."

■ ■ ■ ■ ■

Chapter 1 Conclusion

In any system, including an education system, all aspects of the system are connected. A school, it is often argued, can improve student achievement by focusing on school culture or by improving the facilities or by increasing school spirit. CSLA's experience with school leadership teams, however, indicates that a direct focus on improving student achievement can have a disproportionate impact on other needs of the school. Despite the multitude of demands placed on schools, school leadership teams have a great impact on student achievement and school culture because they focus their work and the work of the school community on developing a supportive, professional environment; building skills and competency; and aligning organizational beliefs, values, and identity with the success generated by the continuous improvement of student achievement.

Build the Team

Never doubt that a small group of thoughtful, committed citizens can change the world. Indeed, it's the only thing that ever has.

— Margaret Mead

LESSON THREE

three

Build Commitment and Focus before the Team Begins Its Work — It Will Save Time

AT A GLANCE

A school leadership team, its school, and its district can forge preliminary understandings that increase the likelihood of the team's success.

This lesson discusses the importance of all parties being clear about the purpose of the team, including the roles and responsibilities of all participants and supporters, before the team begins its work. Issues of contracting are discussed, and brief SLT histories are provided.

The superintendent from the county office of education could provide the funding, and the superintendent from the school district thought that the school's participation in CSLA's School Leadership Team Development Program was a good idea. Thus, on the first day of a two-year seminar series, a group of five teachers from the school showed up. Having been notified the day before the first session that they were a school leadership team, they came in a spirit of goodwill but with considerable confusion about the purpose of the School Leadership Team Development Program. The school principal did not attend. Because they lacked understanding, focus, or commitment, this group never had an impact as a team. The resources of the school were applied ineffectually, potential leaders became skeptical, and the reputation of the program was tarnished.

E ngaging a school leadership team — teachers, the principal, a district office liaison, and perhaps students, parents, and community members — is serious business. Significant amounts of money, time, human energy, and human spirit are required. Of all these resources, human energy and human spirit are the most critical: Neither time nor money can compensate for their absence. Taking care not to squander either energy or spirit, successful SLTs are precise and clear from the beginning about the expectations for the team, the principal, the district, and the School Leadership Team Development Program.

CSLA has learned the value of preliminary work. Over the past ten years, CSLA's process for engaging a school, its district, and a school leadership team in multiyear work to improve student achievement has itself become clearer and more precise. Initially, because CSLA staff could not predict how the School Leadership Team Development Program would be received, we were eager to accept any school interested in participating. School leadership teams began their participation with a wide range of understanding of the program. (The vignette that begins this lesson describes an extreme case during those early days.)

As CSLA staff reflected on the cases of teams that, from the start, failed to thrive, the patterns we discovered led us to initiate an ongoing process to ensure the readiness of teams to begin the program and, thus, the student achievement improvement process. The staff of CSLA's regional School Leadership Centers (SLCs) developed what has come to be known as presession work.

Presession Work

The work that an SLT and CSLA undertake before beginning the School Leadership Team Development Program is presession work. This work is designed to provide contextual support for the eventual work of the SLT. The intended outcomes of presession work are many:

- to make certain that members of the SLT, the principal, the staff of the school, and the district are clear about the direction and purpose of the program;

- to provide the staff of the school with a role in deciding whether to commit to the SLT process; and

- to provide information to the facilitators of the program regarding the school's readiness, specific needs, strengths, and challenges.

Typically, it is the principal who first investigates participation in the School Leadership Team Development Program. The principal may hear about the program through other CSLA programs, word of mouth, CSLA marketing materials, or district leadership. The principal usually contacts the School Leadership Center that serves the school's district or county. This initial conversation usually results in one or more meetings at the school.

The first meeting at the site includes a regional CSLA director and the principal; often, key teachers and a district office representative also attend. The usual goals of such a meeting are to get acquainted and develop a shared understanding of the purposes, logistics, expectations, costs, and theory of action of the School Leadership Team Development Program. The role of the school leadership team — to develop the school's capacity to continuously improve student achievement — is delineated. This first meeting is also to determine whether the program fits the needs of the school. Should this initial group decide that the program has merit for the school, a second meeting is scheduled.

The second meeting usually involves the entire staff and has many of the same purposes as the first meeting. In addition, this meeting provides staff members with the opportunity to subscribe to the principles and ideas of the School Leadership Team Development Program and offer their support for the process. Individual teachers may consider participation on the SLT. The model for continuous improvement of student achievement is presented once again, allowing all involved to understand the focus of the team's work. Based on the information provided in these meetings, the staff members determine whether they will commit to a contract with the School Leadership Team Development Program.

Sometimes it is the district's initiative rather than the principal's that brings CSLA to a school. In such cases, the presession work takes a somewhat different pathway. The initial conversation regarding the School Leadership Team Development Program is held at the district level. An SLC director, the superintendent, and assistant superintendents meet to develop a shared understanding of the purposes, logistics, expectations, costs, and theory of action of the School Leadership Team Development Program. Participants also determine whether the program fits the needs of the district and its schools.

The SLT Contract

Each regional SLC has developed a contract that can be modified to suit an individual district's and SLT's circumstances. This contract describes the roles and responsibilities of the SLC, the SLT, the school staff, and the district office. This agreement puts into writing the understandings that are discussed in the initial meetings; it formalizes the expectations that each contributor agrees to meet. This process of developing a shared understanding and gaining commitment to the process in a written contract has significantly increased the readiness of SLTs to begin their work with precision and focus. (See Appendix C for a sample contract.)

After the contract is signed, some SLCs meet with the principal before the first seminar to discuss the school's student achievement data and possible areas of focus for the SLT. If an SLT does not currently exist, the process of selecting team members is discussed (see Lesson Four). Methods of SLT communication with staff, the availability of time for the SLT to work with staff, and support from teacher associations and district leadership are also discussed.

Because they have been engaged in presession work, the SLTs attend the first seminar session prepared to begin the program work. They come with clarity of purpose; certainty of focus; support from the principal, school staff, and district; and the basic logistics established. From this footing, SLTs can begin immediately to focus on learning how to complete the work they need to do.

A Case in Brief

An SLC met with the district administration and all the district principals in a retreat setting to discuss the contract. The SLC had completed its part of the contract, a description of the services and responsibilities of the SLC; at the retreat, the district and principals added descriptions of their roles and responsibilities. This more complete contract was discussed at the first meeting of the district's school leadership teams. Each team reviewed the agreement forged by the SLC, the district, and their principal, and then added their own responsibilities to the contract. These contracts guided the SLTs' first year of work. Before beginning the second and third years of their participation, the agreements were revisited, revised, and reaffirmed.

four

Pay Attention to Who's on the Team — People Matter

AT A GLANCE

People make a big difference. The membership of the school leadership team has a great influence on the ultimate success of the team.

This lesson considers factors of team membership. The importance of the principal and of district representation are highlighted. Team size, team selection processes, and issues related to parent and student membership are considered. Several brief SLT histories are included.

A rather successful elementary school in a large urban school district included participation in the School Leadership Development Program as part of its school plan. During two whole-staff meetings, the school staff considered whether to participate. Many of the staff were powerful, experienced teachers who had helped to found the school as a magnet two decades earlier. The administration gained a loose agreement from the staff to begin the process. However, when staff selected team members, their lack of commitment was clear. Grade-level groups, the classified staff group, and the teaching specialists each chose a representative to the SLT. Instead of choosing their most effective leaders from across the spectrum, the selections included a teacher brand new to the school, a vociferous veteran, the least experienced teacher in a grade level, and a custodian. The principal, while automatically on the team, was relatively green, with only three years' experience. There was no district representative on the team. The result was an ineffective group that had no impact.

Making a commitment to focus on student achievement and to develop practices that support continuous improvement is a test of any SLT member's leadership skills and dedication. As described in Lesson Two, such a focus will alter the deep structures of a school's culture — its beliefs, values, and identity. Yet leaders must not underestimate the propensity of a system to reject change, to maintain its stability. In short, leaders who push for the re-examination of education practices or beliefs can anticipate that the system will push back at them. Roland Barth (February 2001), for example, warns that resistance will be both passive and active:

> Many teachers report that the greatest obstacle to their leadership comes from colleagues. If they can get by the issues of time, tests, and tight budgets, their reward is the disapprobation of fellow teachers and administrators, who wield an immense power to extinguish a teacher's involvement in school leadership.
>
> There are many reasons why the teacher who would lead encounters resistance from fellow teachers. Opposition often comes in bizarre, enervating, and discouraging forms. Some are passive — inertia, caution, insecurity, primitive personal and interpersonal skills — while others are active. (p. 446)

Characteristics of SLT Members

Members of SLTs must be strong people. The success of their work to improve student achievement depends on their capacity to create conditions that positively influence the work of their colleagues. In documenting CSLA's work with school leadership teams, researchers led by Janet Chrispeels at the University of California, Santa Barbara (UCSB), Gervitz Graduate School of Education reported that the relationship of the team with the staff of the school correlates with changes in the school's teaching and learning practices: The more effective the SLT's relationship with the staff, the more changes in teaching and learning there are, and the more student achievement improves (1999). To be effective, SLT members must be able to develop effective relationships with their colleagues.

SLT members must have an inner strength and sense of purpose that will see them through the inevitable challenges. They must be capable of holding a large vision; they must also be able to understand the details. These teacher leaders must be able to coalesce into a team, as the collective strength, spirit, energy, and purpose of the team will provide support for the often risky work of its members. Thus, members must have or be able to learn effective group participation skills. The views of members of the team need not be alike. In fact, informed, diverse perspectives and multiple views add strength to the team. However, while team members must be able to advocate for their firmly held beliefs and perspectives, they must also know when to yield to the purpose of the team in order for the team to progress.

Including Students, Parents, and Community Members

Some SLTs have made a great effort to include students, parents, and community members on the team (students, typically, are included at the middle school and high school levels). The results have been mixed.

For many students, discussion about the details of CIPP holds little interest. The presence of students on a school leadership team, however, provides a reality check that often has a great influence on staff views. Students' perspectives on the data and their questions and suggestions can lead to breakthroughs in team thinking.

When parents and community members are included on an SLT, they typically demonstrate a strong interest in all areas related to improving student achievement. In some cases, they also bring to the team significant experience, expertise, and background knowledge related to education. In other cases, the team must allocate time to bring these team members up to speed. This necessary process slows the work of the team.

Early SLT efforts to include the voices of students and parents were found to extend the length of time required to build the team's ability to affect the staff. This is not to suggest that such time is not well spent: It might well lead to valuable perspectives and more effective actions. But given today's climate of high-stakes accountability, teams find time to be a critical element. This pressure to show results can work against the desire for fuller inclusion.

Furthermore, depending on the culture of the school, much work might be needed for the teachers and the principal to develop into a team. Issues of trust, history, honesty, hidden agendas, and personal agendas often delay the development of the team. In such cases, the inclusion of students, parents, or community members impedes frank and often emotional discussion, the type of discussion that is better limited to professional colleagues. Based on data gathered from California SLTs, Chrispeels and other UCSB researchers suggest that in these instances, the inclusion of students, parents, or community members might best be delayed (1997).

District Liaison and School Liaison

Teams invariably benefit from ongoing contact with and support from the school district office. In fact, a district liaison to the team or a team liaison to the district is vital to the success of the team. The 1999 Chrispeels UCSB study found that the team's relationship with the district correlated with the team's influence on teaching and learning. This finding led CSLA to provide for the inclusion of a district liaison in all SLT contracts.

The active participation of a district liaison has many positive results:

- The work of the team will be aligned with the direction and focus of the district.

- The district will understand the work of the team and the challenges that it faces.

- The district can offer support through policy, finance, and shared information that can accelerate the work of the team.

- The district will develop a deeper understanding of the context of the school and can take actions for its improvement.

- The district can link the team with resources.

- The district can support continuous improvement by providing the data that the school needs.

- The district liaison will share responsibility for providing appropriate support to the school.

The following example illustrates consistent district knowledge of and support for the efforts of SLTs, with predictably positive results all around:

A Case in Brief

In Sweetwater Union High School District in San Diego County, the school district office initiated the School Leadership Team Development Program for all of its middle schools and high schools. To ensure accurate information from the schools and effective planning of the seminar sessions, each school selected a staff member as a liaison to the district office. These school liaisons meet monthly with the superintendent and area superintendents to reflect on the progress of the teams and the schools, and to influence the content and process of the next seminar session. Area superintendents and school board members attend the seminar sessions in support of the work of the teams.

In contrast, when the district is not knowledgeable about and involved with the goals and work of an SLT, the district and SLT can actually be operating at cross purposes:

A Case in Brief

An elementary school received a five-year grant to restructure the organization. The school began the School Leadership Team Development Program as a way to focus their restructuring work. During the first year, no meetings were held between the SLT and the school district regarding the focus of the team's work. At the end of the first year, those members of the teaching staff who did not wish to take part in the changes planned for the school transferred to other schools. The district policy at the time did not allow the school to interview and select replacement teachers; instead, replacements were assigned on the basis of seniority. Many of the new teachers opposed the vision of the school. Through participating in the distributed leadership processes of the school, these staff members began to alter its direction. At the end of the second year, the principal, still in the midst of this five-year, high-profile effort, was appointed to a position in the district office by a new superintendent. The team faltered under new leadership. The result was factions, mistrust, extreme emotions, declining student achievement, and an ineffective use of resources.

The disappointing results of this elementary school's efforts did not arise solely from the lack of a supportive relationship with the district, but the absence of a liaison between the district and the school leadership team certainly played a role.

Principal's Role in SLT

The principal must be a member of the team and attend all seminar sessions. Without the active participation of the principal at all seminar sessions, the team's ability to plan specific leadership actions is greatly hampered. The time required to brief and gain the support of the principal can be significant. Most SLT contracts state that if the principal is unable to attend an SLT seminar session, the team will be asked to return to their school. (See Lesson Seven for a discussion of the principal's role on the team.)

Selection Process for Staff SLT Members

The process for selecting staff SLT members varies from site to site. Often the principal decides what the selection process will be and bases it on school traditions. In some cases, the principal asks for volunteers and then selects from those who come forward.

In other cases, the principal works with the teachers' association representative or with a group of highly respected teachers to choose who will serve from a list of volunteers. Some principals actively encourage individuals whom they consider to have leadership ability to volunteer.

Sometimes school tradition or context calls for a more formal process. Elections might be held for a representative from each grade level or from each grade-level span, such as primary and intermediate. Teachers might vote by department or by interdisciplinary team unit.

Regardless of the selection process, the question guiding membership selection is about results: Considering the work of the team and the context of the school, who is needed on the team to get the work done? Figure 7 includes criteria that can help answer this question.

Figure 7. Criteria for Selecting SLT Teacher Members

The following criteria can help in the selection of staff to serve on a school leadership team:

- respect for and influence of the teacher among his or her colleagues;
- teacher's knowledge and leadership capacity;
- unique or specialized perspective that the teacher would bring to the team;
- grade-level or content area expertise of the teacher;
- teacher's specialized training (e.g., special education, reading, English language development);
- teacher's relationships with key members of the staff;
- teacher's sense of the history, traditions, and context of the school;
- teacher's aspiration to become an administrator; and
- teacher's ability to lend balance to the makeup of the team.

Blockers as Team Members

It is not uncommon for a teacher who wields significant power and influence to assume the role of a blocker. This person apparently feels that his or her role is to slow down or stop the process of change or to maintain the status quo. In many cases, those charged with the selection of team members confront the question of whether to include a blocker on the team. Some hope that including the blocker will lead this person to develop a deeper understanding of the needs of the school and to shift his or her thinking to become an outspoken supporter of change. Others believe that a blocker requires too much of the group's time and energy, and that scarce resources should not be allocated to the conversion of a blocker.

It is helpful to distinguish between a blocker and a skeptic. A skeptical team member can benefit the team. A skeptic demands that the team think clearly, identifies issues other team members might not consider, and reflects a point of view shared by a predictable portion of the school's staff. A blocker, on the other hand, seeks control and requires endless attention. A blocker's needs are rarely satisfied, and he or she retards or prevents the progress of the team. The inclusion of a blocker on a team rarely benefits the team or the school.

Team Size

The size of the team usually mirrors the size of the school. The typical elementary school team has five or six members. A middle school team, depending on its size and representational structure, may have eight to twelve members. A comprehensive high school may have ten to fifteen members on its SLT.

Several additional factors influence the size of the team: the budget for substitute teachers to replace teacher leaders for seminar days and for intersession work, the availability of substitute teachers, the number of team members needed to be in accord with the representational structure of the school, and the school's notion of the ideal number of individuals who would work efficiently as a team.

Transitions and Planned Rotation of Team Members

The membership of an SLT changes across time. The personal and professional lives of team members will require that some people retire from the team. These transitions are something that teams must take into account in their planning. Although a team's original commitment to the School Leadership Team Development Program is for two or three years, many teams recommit for several additional years.

Even in the case of a well-developed team, a change in membership returns the team to the first step of the process of becoming a team. As described by Margaret Arbuckle and Lynn Murray in *Building Systems for Professional Growth: An Action Guide,* a team proceeds through a four-step sequence in becoming a team: (1) forming, (2) storming, (3) norming, and (4) performing. Each step is characterized by a series of negotiated agreements about roles, relationships, purpose, and processes used by the team. A change in membership returns the team to the forming stage and requires that the team revisit its key understandings — the purpose statement of the team, the operational agreements of the team, and the logistical arrangements for meetings and work. This is also a time for team members to reflect on the history, accomplishments, current goals, and challenges of the team.

Whenever an experienced member leaves and a new member joins the team, the team has important relationship work to do as well. They will want to celebrate the contributions of the departing member and take the time to develop personal relationships with the new member. Many teams stagger their membership terms so that the team is always composed of both experienced and new members. In this way, teams build the leadership capacity and understanding of the SLT process among more staff, relieve long-standing team members of the responsibility of formal leadership, and return experienced SLT members to the staff, thus increasing staff support for the work of the team.

Use Real Work to Build the Team — It's Authentic

AT A GLANCE

When a school leadership team does the authentic work of focusing on student achievement, it can develop all the characteristics of an effective team. It is not necessary for the team to engage in simulations or exercises.

In this lesson, brief SLT histories add specifics to the discussion of authentic work.

"The first thing we do," says Bob Pape, executive director of CSLA's North Bay/Coastal Consortium SLC, "is to have the teachers start collecting data from test scores and in-class assignments. Then we teach them how to analyze the data." This is the process under way for Wilson Elementary School, where the student population includes few students living in poverty and few students who speak English as a second language, but where the Academic Performance Index (API) at one point hovered around 650, which is 150 points below the minimum target for California schools. Team members, who include the principal and a teacher from each grade level, learned to use student achievement data to focus on continuous improvement of student achievement and taught the skills to their colleagues. The school's API has risen to 710. A kindergarten teacher says, "We were suddenly looking at things as professionals. We were looking at data and standards and saying, 'We can do this. This is not a mystery to us.' The process has been empowering. And then once the teachers are empowered, it is really easy for us to turn around and empower our students."

Time spent in school is precious. Time spent with a school leadership team is precious. There is no time to waste! As facilitators of SLT work, CSLA has had to answer this question: What is the most efficient way to develop the SLT into a team that is capable of taking focused action to improve student achievement?

Team building is a small "industry" in the professional development field, with resources ranging from games, simulations, and group challenges to videos of high-performing teams at work. These professional development tools may create a temporary sense of teamwork or help develop insight into what a team of people working together is like, yet they cannot develop a true team. A true team does authentic work in real contexts and makes significant progress toward desired results.

In California, as in other states, the advent of a statewide accountability system for student achievement has clarified the desired results for a school and its leadership team. And with the greater availability of data and the technology to disaggregate, organize, format, and display the data, the authentic work has become clearer. It is in this new context that the old strategies used to build teams can be put on the shelf and teams can be built using the authentic work that they are challenged to do.

SLTs have much authentic work to do and many ways of building the team:

- A team develops a set of agreements regarding how team members will interact. These ground rules serve as a baseline against which team development can be compared at any point in time by any member of the team.

- A team develops a clear and concise purpose statement.

- The team shares the proposed purpose statement with the school staff as part of a report to the staff (SLTs make these reports to staff following each seminar). Armed with comments from the staff, the team makes appropriate modifications and places the purpose statement in the team portfolio.

- Team members develop an understanding of and rotate the roles of facilitator, timekeeper, recorder, and group member.

- In their team discussions, team members practice three elements of coaching: (1) pause, (2) paraphrase, and (3) probe.

- A team collects student achievement data and implements the techniques and skills of data analysis.

- Through the data analysis, a team identifies points of celebration and areas of renewed focus.

- Team members plan meetings of their colleagues using backward design methods.

- At such meetings, team members present the collected student achievement data and teach their colleagues to analyze the data.

- Through data analysis, team members facilitate the work of their colleagues in setting student achievement improvement goals.

The preceding team leadership actions are just a few examples of a team's authentic work. To do this complex work, teamwork is required. The demands of the work mean that the group members must develop their capacity as a team.

A Case in Brief

An elementary school on a year-round schedule planned a set of meetings with teachers from different grade levels to help them develop a deep understanding of what the student achievement data from the SAT 9 and district writing assessments indicated. One team member with strong skills in technology and data analysis assumed responsibility for providing each grade level with the appropriate data in multiple formats. Other team members paired up to design the specifics of the meetings and to plan the facilitation of different parts of the meetings. Yet another team member, with a special interest in the culture and climate of the school, took responsibility for the refreshments and environment of the meeting rooms. Team members set a planning schedule that included opportunities to comment on one another's work before the events. This would allow team members to point out gaps in planning, red flags (warnings), and sweet spots (clever and effective ideas). Following the meetings with teachers, team members gathered to debrief, reflect on what they had learned, discuss what could be improved, and celebrate one another's efforts. This relatively high-achieving school has seen a 5 percent growth in student achievement for three consecutive years.

■ ■ ■ ■ ■

Chapter 2 Conclusion

The success of a team as a team depends on a number of factors. Some of the most critical factors are as follows:

- Quality presession work. This provides clear information and allows the school or district and the team to begin participation in the School Leadership Team Development Program with confidence, a sense of support, a clear direction, and sound relationships with the program facilitators, the staff, and the district.

- Selection of team members. The selection process creates a group that is capable of developing into a team and accomplishing the work at hand. Many factors are considered in this selection process, including a potential team member's sense of the history, traditions, and context of the school. No one selection process is the right process for all schools.

- Use of the important work of the school to build the team. A team can begin at any place in the continuous improvement cycle, but getting to student achievement data sooner rather than later pays off. Use of the school's authentic work can accelerate the development of the team.

Develop Leadership

Improvement...is change with direction, sustained over time, that moves entire systems, raising the average level of quality and performance while at the same time decreasing the variation among units, and engaging people in analysis and understanding of why some actions seem to work and others don't.... Leadership is the guidance and direction of instructional improvement.

— Richard F. Elmore
Building a New Structure for School Leadership

Facilitate the Transition of the Team from Learners to Learners-as-Leaders — It's Huge

AT A GLANCE

By learning to lead the learning of others, members increase their own drive for ongoing learning.

This lesson outlines the learning theory and approaches of the CSLA School Leadership Team Development Program and how leadership teams apply their seminar learning. A research model of the School Leadership Team Development Program shows the correlation of leadership team effectiveness with relationships across an education system and with student achievement.

A middle school SLT reflected on the often traumatic experiences that team members had when sharing their team's work and leading whole-staff meetings. Strategically, they determined that if they could work in pairs and gather their colleagues in smaller groups, they would be better able to communicate with their colleagues, engage their colleagues in work focused on student achievement, and create a more positive climate. This SLT was learning about leading.

Learning and leading are interwoven. A key assumption of the School Leadership Team Development Program's theory of action is that a well-selected team can learn to take leadership actions that affect what individual teachers do in their classrooms, leading to a school's continuous improvement of student achievement. Learning what those actions are and how to implement them means that leadership teams have much to learn — about leading and about facilitating the learning of those being led.

The "What" of Leadership Learning

Even after they have completed the presession work described earlier, team members enter the School Leadership Team Development Program with a range of readiness to engage in continuous improvement. The individual members of the team bring a wide variety of experience, expertise, and knowledge to the team. Many have strengths in curriculum and instruction, classroom management, and content expertise, but few have a deep knowledge of organizational behavior, student data collection and analysis, professional development planning, adult learning theory, or continuous improvement models. Some groups arrive with the attributes of a school leadership team partially developed; other groups are composed of members who have spent little time together.

Each CSLA School Leadership Center (SLC) designs each seminar series to meet the needs of a team and its school, district, and region. There is no single scope and sequence for the School Leadership Team Development Program. However, as outlined in Lessons One and Two, all seminars focus on the phases of the continuous improvement planning process, which includes the introduction of a number of key skills in team development, organizational culture, leadership, systems thinking, research into teaching and learning, and standards-based practice (see Figure 8).

The Conditions for Learning

While two years is usually the minimum commitment an SLT makes for its work with CSLA, institutionalizing the work of an SLT requires more than two years. For this reason, some schools authorize an extension of the two-year agreement one or more times. And some SLCs require a minimum three-year commitment from the start.

The design of the School Leadership Team Development Program is guided by the CSLA learning theory (see Figure 9) and a pattern of seminar learning that includes reflection, new learning, action planning and sharing, followed by between-seminar (intersession) implementation.

Figure 8. Leadership Skills Needed by SLTs

CSLA designs its work with school leadership teams to address a range of skills and considerations that contribute to team success.

Team Development

- team ground rules
- decision-making and consensus
- team roles: facilitator, recorder, timekeeper, and group member
- coaching skills
- multiple intelligence and cognitive style assessments
- problem analysis
- meeting planning (backward design)
- brainstorming and prioritizing
- skillful discussion, dialogue, and advocacy
- use of large wall templates (histomaps, context maps, graphic game plans, visioning templates, program profiles, and program cycles)
- reflection on action, including assessment of action density
- monitoring team development
- developing relationships with site and district colleagues, students, and parents
- reflective protocol
- professional development planning

Organizational Culture

- assessment of readiness
- norms, values, beliefs, and assumptions
- rituals and celebrations
- organizational behavior
- culture-shaping tools
- culture-assessment tools
- organizational structure and governance

Leadership

- distributed leadership
- teacher leadership
- role of the principal
- role of the district
- facilitation skills
- symbolic actions

Systems Thinking

- complexity or chaos theory
- self-organizing systems
- value of information, relationships, and identity
- systems tools (ladder of inference, five whys, fishbowl, multiple-perspective wheels, dialogue, and metaphor)
- double-loop learning

Teaching and Learning Research

- program selection strategies
- implementation strategies
- assessment strategies
- evaluation strategies

Standards-Based Practice

- backward mapping of curriculum and instruction to standards
- developing standards-based formative assessments

Figure 9. The CSLA Learning Theory

The CSLA learning theory states that learning is best facilitated

- when tasks are meaningful to the learner because they emerge from authentic issues and problems;
- when learners construct their own meaning and apply, reflect upon, and receive comments on applications in a real-world setting;
- in an environment that is absent of threat and promotes high challenge, intellectual rigor, and motivated inquiry;
- when learners are empowered to use their personal strengths and hold themselves and one another accountable for appropriate action;
- when learners are viewed as a rich resource, are valued for their diversity, and interact collaboratively as a learning community;
- through in-depth, problem-solving projects approached from a variety of perspectives; and
- when the learner is personally connected to the content and context of learning.

Seminars are held five or six times a year, with five or six "intersessions" of four to seven weeks between seminars. Typically seminars are scheduled with five to ten SLTs meeting together. Each day of the seminar is divided among three major topics:

- reflection on intersession action (including sharing among teams, comments, and coaching);

- new content (including conceptual knowledge and leadership processes and skills); and

- team planning of intersession work, preparation, and practice (including the integration of team skills practice and sharing among teams, comments, and coaching).

With the recognition that much leadership consists of the use of appropriate processes, SLCs have gradually increased the portion of seminar agendas devoted to teaching and rehearsing leadership practices. Because most of the interaction of an SLT with staff is professional development that is carried out through doing the authentic work of the school, the leadership processes can be compared to instructional practices in a classroom. The SLT is a team of educators planning authentic curriculum and instruction designed to create new ways of thinking and practice; in this case, their students are their colleagues. While team members plan meetings designed to attain clearly identified outcomes, they consider the knowledge that their colleagues currently have, their colleagues' possible misperceptions, and their colleagues' attitudes, personal interests, and needs.

The School Leadership Team Development Program is a continuous improvement cycle in itself. At each seminar, team members review data and set a goal for the work that they will do next with their staff. A plan of action in the form of a graphic game plan is developed, and team members design appropriate intersession work to put the plan into action. SLTs share their plans for intersession work with other SLTs in order to make a symbolic commitment to the work and to solicit comments and support from other SLTs. Comments and support can take the form of verbal encouragement, fine-tuning suggestions, or warnings based on other SLTs' experiences. At the subsequent seminar session, team members reflect on the action taken, consider the results of the action, identify lessons and effective practices, and add artifacts to the team portfolio. Each team shares their reflection with all SLTs, thus helping to build a repertoire of best practices.

Once a year, SLCs hold a one-day summative seminar. Some SLCs schedule this day at the end of a school year; others wait until the fall, when all data are available for consideration. For this summative, taking-stock day, team members prepare for a reflective protocol focused on (1) the progress of their work to build a school's capacity to practice continuous improvement and (2) the progress of students toward the student achievement improvement goal. Team members reflect on evidence of progress and present it to their colleague teams. Their colleague teams, in turn, provide affirmation of the SLT's work and ask questions to encourage the team's ever-deeper consideration of their practice and the impact of their efforts. This closing ritual is also the beginning of a new cycle of work. The cyclical nature of the endeavor is an important aspect of the work of the School Leadership Team Development Program.

In addition to the seminar program itself, SLTs benefit from their relationship with CSLA program facilitators, who monitor the needs of each team and intervene with appropriate facilitation support. This support can occur within the seminar; for example, CSLA facilitators often model methods during a seminar for moving a team's discussion forward. Facilitation can also occur at a school site during the intersession, where program facilitators can provide high levels of support.

Teams progress at different rates. It has been critical that CSLA facilitators acknowledge this fact and create a totally noncompetitive seminar environment. Norms of collegiality, collaboration, mutual celebration of progress, support, and sharing are essential to this work.

In the early stages of a team's development, the team may benefit from the intense, frequent, and direct involvement of a facilitator who takes the role of a mentor. Teams with high levels of readiness, including a highly skilled principal (see Lesson Seven), skilled teacher leaders who see their leadership role clearly (see Lesson Eight), and an organizational culture that invites collaboration and a clear focus on improvement, require less direct facilitator support; they benefit from the more open-ended support of an individual serving as a coach.

The Application of Learning

The School Leadership Team Development Program research conducted by Janet Chrispeels and her UCSB colleagues shows that the most immediate application of the content, skills, and processes from the program happens within the SLT itself and within the classrooms of the teachers who are SLT members (1998). As open and honest relationships develop among team members, they come to feel at ease practicing their new skills and processes with one another and then later in their classrooms. And as SLT members learn more about student assessment, analysis of data, and the nuances of a standards-based system, they find ways to use the information with their own students. The transfer of content, skills, and processes is relatively easy: The teacher makes sense of them, and his or her classroom practices begin to change.

The use of the new content, skills, and processes with the entire school staff, however, is a different story. The complexities of the school — the diverse views, interpersonal relationships, organizational history, school culture, patterns of organizational structure, and district and community context — may mean that the application of SLT content, skills, and processes is a relatively easy task or an overwhelming task. And even a school with the most favorable combination of conditions requires that the individual members of the SLT and the team as a whole perform leadership tasks that are both unfamiliar and challenging. An adverse combination of conditions in a school can mean that the progress of the team is very slow. Within a cohort of SLTs, teams will be able to apply their learning with their entire staffs at different rates.

As team members develop their capacity and confidence to take leadership actions, they intervene with staff in ways that improve the relationship of the SLT with the staff. Team members become more precise in planning, designing, and orchestrating their interactions with staff. Their sophistication increases. Their reflection becomes increasingly accurate. They anticipate and consider an ever-increasing set of variables; they develop the facilitation capacity, skills, and processes for a multitude of situations. Correspondingly, the staff develop confidence in the team's leadership, and once the members of the team show how student achievement has improved at the monthly data analysis and corrective action meetings, a cycle of positive reinforcement begins.

From the start, the School Leadership Team Development Program focuses on the relationship of the SLT with the staff. The presession work described in Lesson Three leads the SLT to begin its work with clear, open, and honest relationships. As team members leave their campus for seminar days, however, some stay-behind staff members will question what is going on. To minimize the spread of misinformation and hearsay, intersession work always includes the team members' report to the staff about the most recent seminar agenda and the work that they completed. SLTs practice ongoing, open, accurate, and transparent communication to assure staff that team members have no secret agenda, that team members are not becoming part of the administration, and that the work of the team focuses on what was promised by the contract and described in the presession meetings. The practice of reporting is the first and most basic interaction between team members and their colleagues. Comprehensive, forthcoming reports set the tone for other team-staff interactions and help satisfy more cynical staff members about the value of the SLT work.

To move beyond simply reporting to the staff, SLT members must learn to apply processes, skills, and tools that have been modeled for them and that they have practiced as part of their seminar work. Prioritization practices, histomaps, action plans, and context maps are examples of some of the processes and tools that SLT members work to master. Team members use the seminar session as a design laboratory, preparing themselves to use the appropriate tools on site. When team members face a special design challenge, CSLA facilitators or members of other SLTs lend their expertise or coach the team through the design of a particularly critical meeting.

Teams always debrief their intersession activities with their SLT cohorts at the beginning of each seminar session. Lessons learned and best practices are listed. This process of reflection on action is key to improving meeting design and building a team's sense of efficacy. One SLT's successes are celebrated by all SLTs, for all SLT work is done in an effort to meet implementation criteria: SLT work is not a competition among teams.

Teams are able to gauge their own growth and development with the School Leadership Team Program Impact Questionnaire created by the UCSB researchers (see Appendix D). Some SLTs complete the survey in an early seminar session to obtain baseline data for the school. All SLTs complete the survey at the end of a program year. The data are then summarized and reported to each team, and teams use the data to set priorities for improvement in the upcoming year.

SLTs really can make a difference. The UCSB researchers have found that the improvement of student achievement in a school correlates with the influence of the SLT on teaching and learning in classrooms. The influence of the SLT on teaching and learning in classrooms, in turn, correlates with the quality of relationships that the SLT has with both the school staff and the district office, and with the use of data by the school. And a single factor correlates with the ability of the team to have good relationships with both the school staff and the district office: the level of development of the SLT as a team (see Figure 10).

The Ongoing Learning of Leaders

As SLT members begin to take a more active leadership role with their colleagues, their need for ongoing learning becomes more important. Team members' involvement in the authentic, real-life work of improving teaching and learning creates in them a need to know. Team members want to know more about the school staff and more about their district and its policies. They want to build their skills of facilitation, coaching, designing meetings, and designing professional development. Their need for specific data increases as new questions attract attention. Information and the skills to involve students, parents, and community members in the school become more important to them. They want to develop a deeper understanding of systems theory, organizational behavior, and change. Methods for researching effective teaching and learning strategies are more important to them. They seek ideas for maintaining progress in developing a more productive school culture, and they seek the opinions of other SLTs. Learning and leading only become more and more interwoven.

Figure 10. Factors That Correlate with an SLT's Influence on Teaching, Learning, and Student Achievement

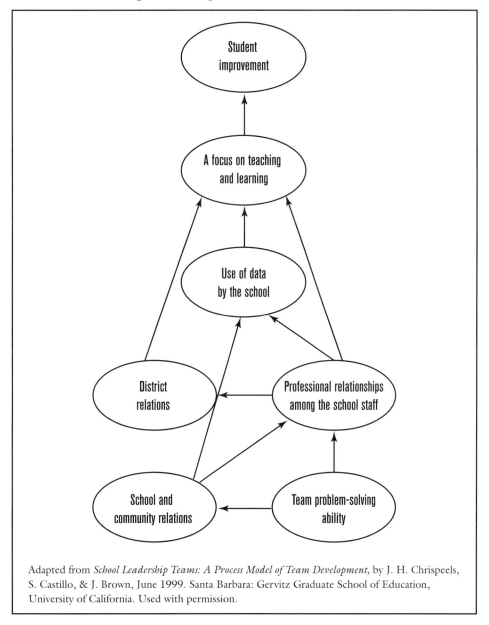

Adapted from *School Leadership Teams: A Process Model of Team Development,* by J. H. Chrispeels, S. Castillo, & J. Brown, June 1999. Santa Barbara: Gervitz Graduate School of Education, University of California. Used with permission.

A Case in Brief

The principal of an elementary school serving mostly middle-class students engaged her school in the School Leadership Team Development Program for four years. At that point, because the principal was satisfied with the capacity of her school, the team did not re-enroll in the program. A year later, the principal chose to return to the program because the team missed the benefits of the collegial support of the other SLTs and the rhythm of the program.

LESSON SEVEN

Ensure Principal Commitment — It's Not Optional

AT A GLANCE

The leadership support and active participation of the principal on the school leadership team is a must.

In this lesson, the principal's role in creating "structural tension" is discussed and brief SLT histories point out the importance of a principal's commitment to the SLT.

The principal of a rural high school serving Spanish-speaking students of poverty forms a school leadership team. Its members include the principal; representative teachers, classified staff, parents, and students from each grade level; an assistant superintendent; and a member of the city council. Together, they turn their attention to improving the reading capability of all students, stewarding the implementation of strategies and programs to meet the needs of each student and, simultaneously, creating communities of practice among the staff. State test scores increase significantly for two years in a row. There is still much to do, but the principal has created a team as devoted as he is to continuing the work.

Most educators recognize the role of the principal as a visionary leader. Most also assume that the principal would lead the implementation of any school improvement effort. In the School Leadership Team Development Program, these roles also involve the principal in facilitating the leadership of others, especially the members of the school leadership team. The principal's participation on the SLT and in support of the SLT is not optional. At the same time, CSLA recognizes the importance of building support for principals' own development into its leadership team development program.

Leading toward a Shared Vision from a Shared Reality

The principal has the authority to lead the development of a powerful vision for a school — or not. In most cases, it is the principal who initiates a school's involvement with the School Leadership Team Development Program and the creation of a school leadership team. Ultimately, the success of a school leadership team depends on the principal's vision and the principal's participation on the team.

This is not to say that the principal can succeed alone. As the principal's role becomes increasingly complex, he or she simply cannot do the leadership work of a school single-handedly. The role of the principal increasingly requires facilitating the leadership of others. According to Ann Lieberman and Lynne Miller in *Teachers — Transforming Their World and Their Work*, as the work of the principal has changed, so have the strategies for successful leadership:

> *What is required is a new kind of leadership, principals who are willing to commit to leading for student accomplishment, for organizational health, for professional learning, and for long-range and deep improvements. These leaders work seriously to support the transformation of schooling and teaching and understand the importance of helping to build a learning community that includes all teachers and students. These are not "Lone Rangers" who depend on charisma and individual genius to transform schools. Rather, they are collaborative learners and teachers who advocate for democratic principles. They work diligently with their faculty and their community to make bold visions a reality. (p. 40)*

For the principal, making bold visions a reality means putting the power of structural tension into play. As discussed in Lesson One, once identified, the structural tension between a school's current reality and where it wants to be is a powerful force.

The principal's first responsibility in this regard is to define a personally held vision for the school and refer to a number of data sources to develop a clear picture of current reality. The principal then shares this vision and information with others, giving colleagues an opportunity to feel the potential for improvement. It is not the job of the principal to impose his or her vision on the school. Instead, the principal's skill as a leader allows others to develop their own visions for the future and their own understandings of current reality — their own feelings of structural tension.

From these individual visions and understandings, the group works to develop a shared vision, a shared understanding of current reality, and a shared sense of structural tension. The more congruent individuals' feelings of structural tension, the more powerful the group's drive to resolve discrepancies will be.

An effective principal understands this and provides opportunities for school leadership team members to formulate a shared vision that captures the passionately held, common views of the team. Team members use dialogue to explore the assumptions that underlie individuals' belief systems. They identify common ground and a common purpose. They read various perspectives on education issues and discover where they and the authors think alike and where they differ. Team members practice effective communication strategies: skillful discussion, dialogue, advocacy, and coaching. These actions are part of the storming and norming phases of becoming a team. The team's creation of a shared vision of the future of the school is a significant step in creating shared structural tension.

The principal also makes sure the SLT understands the school's current reality. Teams learn skills to analyze data and engage in dialogue about the meaning of standardized test scores, demographic data, district achievement data, whole-school data, disaggregated data, longitudinal data, snap-shot data, anecdotal data, and observational data. These analyses and discussions help to establish the team's view of current reality, which, in combination with their shared vision, leads to the development of the team's shared structural tension and sense of urgency to resolve the tension.

And just as the principal cannot be a Lone Ranger, so a team cannot be a posse deputized by the sheriff-principal. After the team has worked through these processes to develop shared structural tension, the staff as a whole must work through the same processes.

The effective principal then provides another form of support. Structural tension can be resolved in one of two ways — by moving the current state of reality toward the vision held by the group or by lowering expectations, limiting the vision to more closely match the current state of reality. It is the principal's role to ensure that the team not back off from the original vision but develop strategies to achieve the vision.

A principal also supports the work of the SLT by maintaining the school's focus on the gap between the vision and the reality. The principal does this by sharing the vision of the school at every opportunity. The principal also makes sure that data are shared openly among all the school's communities. Information about progress and the remaining challenge flows freely. And the principal makes it clear that lowering expectations to reduce structural tension would be a less than honorable resolution of the tension: It would mean selling out some of the students.

The principal maintains a focus on the vision, on the student improvement achievement goal, and on concrete and time-specific movement toward the goal. The attainment of a goal is cause for celebration — measurable progress has been made toward achieving the vision. The principal sees to it that these celebrations of progress are ritualized and that the team's role in the school's success is highly visible.

Facilitating the Leadership of Others

To build leadership within a school leadership team, the principal uses many strategies and skills. Foremost, the principal models respect for team members and for their time. Team meeting agendas, for example, are designed by the team and not the principal. The principal makes time available for the team to successfully complete their work and hires substitute teachers to relieve the time pressure. The principal demonstrates genuine appreciation for the contributions and efforts of the team. Disagreements are seen as productive. The principal assumes that the intent behind any disagreement is to achieve the vision and is not a personal attack. The principal is fully engaged with the team, and shows it by keeping his or her commitments to work with the team, participating in reflection with the team, and identifying both successful and unsuccessful team actions, openly learning from them.

In *Learning by Heart*, Roland Barth identifies a number of principal behaviors that can build a culture of teacher leadership:

- Expecting *and inviting teacher leadership;*

- Relinquishing *some of their authority to teacher leaders;*

- Entrusting *teachers when the going gets tough;*

- Empowering *teachers to address problems before a solution has been determined;*

- Including *teachers in leadership roles who indicate interest in a particular challenge, whether they are experienced leaders or not;*

- Protecting *the leadership actions of teachers from assault by their peers;*

- Sharing Responsibility for Failure, *which results in increased collegiality, safety, trust, and higher morale; and*

- Giving Recognition *for teachers' successful leadership actions.* (pp. 109–113)

Each of these strategies for building leadership calls for the principal to exhibit considerable trust and patience. This would be challenging even if a school were not experiencing structural tension. By definition, however, the role of the school leadership team is to create structural tension! The resulting sense of urgency is felt keenly by the principal. In California, for example, if an underperforming school fails to make progress, the state's accountability system requires that the principal be reassigned.

Unfortunately, this sense of urgency can result in unproductive behavior on the part of the principal. According to Barth (February 2001), the principal can be a barrier to the development of the leadership of others:

> *It is disheartening that many teachers experience their school administrator, and especially their principal, as an obstacle to their leadership aspirations. They see principals holding tightly and jealously onto power, control, and the center stage....*
>
> *And it is risky for a principal to share leadership with teachers. Since principals will be held accountable for what others do, it is natural that they want evidence in advance that those they empower will get the job done well. Principals are also mindful of how much care, feeding, and handholding must go into helping the teacher leader. Given their own time crunches, many principals believe that it is more efficient to make decisions by themselves.... (p. 447)*

Given all the demands on them, it is not uncommon for principals to want to dominate the team. The principal has so much to do and so little time that he or she may try to make team members into converts through a barrage of principal talk and by allowing only shallow processing of ideas. When this happens, however, it ultimately retards the development of the team. It sends a message that the views of the team members are less valuable than the principal's, it limits the perspective and range of options available, and it prevents others on the team from developing leadership skills.

In *Building Leadership Capacity in Schools*, Linda Lambert reflects on the challenges facing the principal intent on facilitating the leadership of others:

> *It is more difficult to build leadership capacity among colleagues than to tell colleagues what to do. It is more difficult to be full partners with other adults engaged in hard work than to evaluate and supervise subordinates.*
>
> *This hard work requires that principals and teachers alike serve as reflective, inquiring practitioners who can sustain real dialogue and can seek outside feedback to assist with self-analysis. These learning processes require finely honed skills in communication, group process facilitation, inquiry, conflict mediation, and dialogue. (p. 24)*

The net result of this hard work is a stronger school. The School Leadership Team Development Program is designed specifically to provide the kind of feedback Lambert calls for in helping principals, and all SLT members, develop these collaborative leadership skills.

Support for Principals

In addition to the support principals receive as SLT members, they often benefit from individual support — as soon as an SLT is formed. Many principals, despite the presession work, have a limited understanding of the importance of their support for the SLT and what the SLT process will demand of them. In many cases, they enter the process intuitively, thinking, "This feels right," and the process teaches them what kind of support to lend the SLT. This is a classic case of "Fire, ready, aim!" Many principals require support during their transition from manager of the status quo to leader of a collaborative, adaptive, democratic, inclusive, and focused school.

A Case in Brief

A new principal joined a school leadership team between the team's first and second years. The team, having grown considerably in their first year of participation, had become very clear about the needs of their students, the school's student achievement goal, and how they could provide leadership to their colleagues. Unaware of how to tap into this leadership and uncomfortable with receiving coaching in his first principalship, the principal felt challenged by the teachers' leadership and so withdrew the team from the School Leadership Team Development Program.

CSLA's regional School Leadership Centers (SLCs) provide a range of support for principals in transition. Some SLCs offer periodic breakfast meetings for SLT principals. In this informal setting, principals share their individual challenges, ideas, and support. Other SLCs provide a content and process preview of an upcoming seminar. This allows principals to anticipate possible issues and roadblocks. SLC directors serve as on-site facilitators of teams completing intersession work. Face-to-face, telephone, and online coaching support for both the team and the principal are made available. CSLA's Network of Educational Coaches provides quality coaching support to principals and teams. In some cases, experienced SLT principals are paired with novice SLT principals to provide coaching. Other SLCs debrief principals immediately after a seminar session, allowing principals to discuss how they can support the team's intersession work. During seminar sessions, a principal may meet with a colleague to discuss challenges and receive suggestions or informal coaching. SLCs that work with a district that has many SLTs collaborate with the district to plan the district's support of principals.

An important tool that SLC coaches can use with principals is the School Leadership Team Implementation Continuum (see Appendix E). Developed by the UCSB researchers with input from CSLA, this survey, which is completed by each team member annually, is a rubric that assesses all aspects of a team's development, including the principal's relationship to the SLT, school norms of collaboration, and capacity building. By helping a principal analyze the collected data, a coach can encourage a principal to go slowly enough to build the team's capacity to lead — so that in the long run the team will function efficiently and quickly.

Develop Teacher Leadership —
It Affects Teaching and Learning

AT A GLANCE

The leadership of the principal, although necessary, is not sufficient.

In this lesson, the critical importance of developing teacher leadership is discussed. Examples of teacher leadership actions are shared.

Some staff members from a school with an SLT began to question the impact of their SLT. Despite the fact that the SLT made regular reports to the staff and organized and facilitated small meetings, some staff questioned whether the school's resources were being used well. The team created a two-year summary of its work, using the "Documenting Team Progress and Learnings" reflection tool (see Appendix F). Team members enlarged this reflection tool so that it was a highly visible wall chart that chronicled their work and its impact on the school. This summary of team actions impressed and satisfied the vast majority of the staff. The summary also provided an effective report to the district's board of education.

Just as the principal has a role in facilitating the development of SLT members' leadership capacity, it is the role of SLT members to facilitate the professional development of their school colleagues. Teachers who serve on the school leadership team have the opportunity to increase the effectiveness of staff throughout the building.

Leading Collegial Professional Development

At the heart of the SLT work — developing the school's capacity to engage in the process of continuous improvement of student achievement — are monthly data analysis and corrective action meetings (see Lessons One and Two for details about the continuous improvement cycle and especially the feedback phase). SLT members plan and facilitate these monthly meetings for small groups of staff, such as grade-level or department teams, who share a common focus and student achievement improvement goal.

Planning and facilitating these consistent, focused, and embedded professional development activities for their school colleagues involves what Bruce Joyce and Beverly Showers describe in *Student Achievement Through Staff Development* as the duties of "active formal leadership":

1. *Organizing the faculty into study groups and coaching teams; meeting with those teams and facilitating their activities.*

2. *Organizing a staff-development/school-improvement council to coordinate activities, select priorities, and ensure facilitation of clinical and systemic components.*

3. *Arranging for time for the collaborative study of teaching and the implementation of curricular and instructional innovations.*

4. *Becoming knowledgeable about training and the options for school improvement.... Ensuring that the staff is knowledgeable.*

5. *Participating in training and the implementation of collective and systemic initiatives. Knowledgeability is the key here, for an in-depth understanding of innovations in curriculum and instruction is necessary to plan facilitation.*

6. *Continuously assessing the educational climate of the school, feeding information and perspective to the faculty for use in decision making about possible areas for study and improvement. (pp. 19–20)*

Of all these activities, the capacity of teacher leaders to facilitate small-group meetings of their colleagues can be an especially limiting factor. University teacher preparation programs rarely address the development of such skills. An important function of the SLT is to support members in building such leadership skills.

This happens indirectly when teachers are able to participate on a well-functioning SLT, one that promotes high levels of trust and open dialogue and that capitalizes on a common language and a shared purpose. This experience of frank and safe conversation is a model for teacher leaders of what they want to achieve in the monthly data analysis and corrective action meetings they facilitate for small groups of teachers.

In addition, teacher leaders focus directly on the skills of leading such meetings. These data analysis and corrective action meetings necessarily reduce the privacy of teacher practice, requiring greater trust, honesty, and openness on the part of teachers, and an increased willingness on their part to adjust instructional practice. Facilitating the development of deeper professional relationships among teachers, which is necessary for such a close examination of the impact of their work, demands significant skill, confidence, and commitment from the facilitator.

Most SLCs provide instruction, tools, models, practice time, and coaching to help SLT members develop the skills and confidence to plan and facilitate such meetings, and to help them take the leadership actions described by Joyce and Showers. For example, one School Leadership Center worked with a district's school leadership teams about ways to share teacher-specific data. The district has a highly developed capacity to provide data about students' progress toward meeting standards and provides all of its SLTs with individual student benchmark writing results, organized by teacher, three times a year. Each SLT must develop ways of sharing these data at the school without provoking a defensive response from those teachers whose students show unsatisfactory progress. Team discussions about how to do this focused on the culture of the school and considered the following questions:

- How can we present these data in a way that elicits productive responses from those needing to improve?

- How can we increase the level of trust and openness to negative data?

- What relationships do we need among ourselves?

- How will we organize and facilitate meetings that share these data?

In addition to help from staff at the School Leadership Centers, teachers on the team can also expect the support of their fellow team members in developing their leadership capabilities. For example, in planning team leadership actions, teachers sometimes assume roles with which they have experience, but frequently they must take on unfamiliar roles that stretch their personal capacity. In such cases, team members develop strategies together and coach one another. Highly developed teams strategically and purposefully place team members in "stretch" situations, and then provide them with the support to see them successfully through the task. Teacher leaders teach one another to complete the authentic work of the team successfully.

Continuous improvement affords other opportunities for teacher leadership. Ad hoc committees might form to complete specific tasks. Teachers, classified staff, and community members might investigate programs and strategies that could help meet the school's student achievement improvement goal. Or an SLT committee seeking to understand the degree of implementation of a reading program might administer a survey to parents and students and report back to the SLT. These opportunities for distributed leadership increase the capacity of the school to complete a wide variety of tasks clearly focused on improving student achievement.

Building Schoolwide Agency

Reflection is built into any continuous improvement model and is crucial to the work of school leadership teams. The SLCs support the SLTs' regular and purposeful reflection on their own actions. Reflection serves as a ritual of learning and celebration, leads to more effective future actions, and documents the actions taken, reminding all interested parties of the work accomplished and the impact of the team.

Perhaps the most important reason for the team's regular practice of reflection on action is the fact that it helps team members identify and discuss the team's successes and any individual member's successes, both large and small. Highlighting successes helps build team members' feelings of agency, a belief that their actions make a difference.

The importance of *feeling* successful to *being* successful is recognized in the cognitive coaching model developed by Art Costa and Robert Garmston:

> *Charles Garfield (1986), in his ongoing study of peak performers, has found [that one] element that stands out clearly among peak performers is their virtually unassailable belief in the likelihood of their own success. (p. 13)*

It may well be that for school leadership team members, feelings of agency, combined with the feelings of urgency generated from a shared sense of structural tension, is the combination that propels them to success. In *Change Forces: The Sequel,* for example, Michael Fullan cites Lorna Earl and Linda Lee's experience with the Manitoba School Improvement Program. Earl and Lee argue that agency, along with urgency, "together generate more energy leading to consolidation, reflection, celebration and the capacity to push even deeper in a further spiral of reform activity."

Thus, when SLT members engage in regular and purposeful reflection on the leadership actions that they have taken, the multiple positive impacts they are able to recognize can sustain the work of the team even in tough times.

A Case in Brief

After seven months of work, members of one SLT were struggling with their collective sense of impact. At an SLT seminar, they were asked to create a visual display – a timeline – of every action that they had taken as a team since the team had formed. As one team member facilitated the reflection, another served as the graphic recorder, noting everything the team could recall on a large wall template. The team members dug into old agendas, examined charts, and called to mind actions taken months before. The team members identified key learnings and big ideas. As they reported to other teams in the room, their sense of accomplishment was visible, and their impact on their school was obvious. They decided that this process would be appropriate work for grade-level teams and departments also.

■ ■ ■ ■ ■

Chapter 3 Conclusion

A school leadership team's ability to exert leadership in order to improve student achievement depends on its ability to deal positively with many interrelated issues. These are summarized below:

- School leadership team members must master key concepts and skills and then learn to use them appropriately in their school's context.

- Learning to lead takes several years and is achieved at different rates by different individuals and teams.

- Team development is facilitated by team members' reflection on action, mastery of new skills and processes, and careful implementation of new skills.

- A team influences student achievement by influencing the teaching and learning that occur within classrooms. A team's ability to affect teaching and learning positively is enhanced by team members' good relationships with their teacher and district office colleagues and the school's capacity to use data. And team members' good relationships with their teacher and district office colleagues are directly related to the state of development of the team.

- The principal supports the team through using time in a symbolic way, maintaining a focus, creating structural tension (urgency), and supporting the growth of the team and its individual members.

- Teacher leadership is vital to the improvement of student achievement. Teacher leaders regularly meet with small groups of colleagues to deprivatize practice and work on the collaborative development of curriculum and instructional strategies that meet the needs of all learners.

- Reflection is integral to continuous improvement and to the development of team and staff feelings of agency.

Create Support

The central office personnel and school leadership have to be closely connected to build shared understandings about the importance of staff development and to ensure that it is focused properly.

— Bruce Joyce and
Beverly Showers
Student Achievement Through Staff Development

Align the Support of the District — It's Systemic

AT A GLANCE

The district, its schools, and their leadership teams exist in an interconnected network.

This lesson describes the district's necessary awareness of and support for school leadership teams. Brief SLT histories illustrate that support from the district can accelerate the teams' work and the improvement of student achievement at local school sites.

A Southern California elementary school district was concerned. Half of its schools were performing above the state average, but the other half were designated "underperforming." The district's entire management team met with CSLA staff at the regional School Leadership Center for two days to focus on the needs of the district's nineteen underperforming schools. The superintendent was determined to develop strategies to provide active support to these schools. As a team, district leadership staff shared their understandings of each of the underperforming schools. They examined their shared views on the quality of the staff, the leadership capacity of the principal, funding sources, curriculum and instruction, parental involvement, characteristics and needs of the student population, professional development, and building maintenance. It was the first time that they had met as a group to develop a shared understanding of their neediest schools. They selected ten underperforming schools to invite to apply for participation in the School Leadership Team Development Program, along with a district team. All ten schools applied, and the district selected six to pilot the strategy. With these six schools, the School Leadership Team Development Program focused on the continuous improvement of student achievement, and the district team attended each seminar day in support of the work of the SLTs. In one year, two schools made such dramatic progress that they were replaced by two other underperforming schools. Two years later, four of the schools had made consistent improvement each year and were no longer categorized as underperforming. The other two schools had mixed results. Looking at the performance of the group of pilot schools, the district decided to involve all of its underperforming schools in the School Leadership Team Development Program.

Once a school agrees to participate in a program of continuous improvement of student achievement, what does support from the district look like?

Defining District Support

Support from the district does not mean that the district tells the school, its principal, or the team what to do. Support from the district means that the district provides a focus, coherence, time, a cyclic rhythm of inquiry, professional development targeted toward building the capacity of the school to continuously improve, and a strong accountability system for the principal and the teachers.

This kind of support combines top-down and bottom-up change strategies, recognizing that while a district may compel a school to work with a change agent, the School Leadership Team Development Program, for example, and may institute a strong accountability system, schools are "learning organizations." As Peter Senge says in *The Fifth Discipline,*

> *While traditional organizations require management systems that control people's behavior, learning organizations invest in improving the quality of thinking, the capacity for reflection and team learning, and the ability to develop shared visions and shared understandings of complex business issues. It is these capabilities that will allow learning organizations to be both more locally controlled and more well coordinated than their hierarchical predecessors. (p. 287)*

School leadership teams are a powerful complement to this kind of organizational structure, yet in many cases, these teams have never considered what district support should be available to them. Some School Leadership Centers (SLCs) engage the team in identifying exactly what support they need from the district. This discussion is often convened in the presence of the district liaison (see below), who can clarify perceptions and respond to the team's request for support.

In general, the kind of support that the district provides is the same kind of support that the principal provides — help to generate and resolve structural tension. The district establishes a clear set of expectations for the school, the principal, and the teachers, but also enables the school and its staff to create their own vision for the school. The district provides the data and processes that help the team develop a shared understanding of current reality. The district also provides professional development support: strategies, practices, tools, and processes that can be used to resolve the structural tension. It is also important for the district to develop ways to celebrate progress while holding people appropriately accountable if progress is lacking.

This overall approach aims for distributed leadership — across the district and across the local sites. In *Building a New Structure for School Leadership*, Richard Elmore points out why distributed leadership makes for a stronger learning organization:

> *Distributed leadership does not mean that no one is responsible for the overall performance of the organization. It means, rather, that the job of administrative leaders is primarily about enhancing the skills and knowledge of people in the organization, creating a common culture of expectations around the use of those skills and knowledge, holding the various pieces of the organization together in a productive relationship with each other, and holding individuals accountable for their contributions to the collective result. (p. 17)*

Policy Support

In addition to creating a district culture that supports distributed leadership, the district can institute policies designed specifically to support the functioning of its school leadership teams. The district can involve the school board in approving participation in the School Leadership Team Development Program, it can provide for liaison between the district and its teams, and it can adopt SLT-friendly policies for selecting and assigning principals.

School Board Resolution

In the past decade, CSLA's School Leadership Centers have become increasingly sophisticated in their development of district support for SLTs. If a school is to participate in the School Leadership Team Development Program, then the school board must pass a resolution supporting the work of the team. This resolution usually guarantees the availability of substitutes for the teacher leaders and active district-level involvement.

District Liaison to the Team and Team Liaison to the District

Data collected by researchers at the University of California, Santa Barbara, about the School Leadership Team Development Program, as well as other research evaluating school restructuring efforts, indicate that the supportive role of the district is even more vital than previously realized. In response to this finding, the SLCs developed an SLT contract that requires the active participation of a district liaison to the SLT.

The role of the liaison is to participate with the team during seminar sessions and intersession work in order to understand the school's specific challenges as the SLT implements the details of the continuous improvement planning process. The liaison communicates with the district specific support needed by the team from the district; he or she often can clear away district obstacles to the team's work.

The district liaison role can be filled by a person in one of many different positions in the district office. In large districts, the director responsible for the school or an area superintendent often serves as the liaison. In smaller districts, an assistant superintendent for curriculum and instruction or even the superintendent may provide the direct support. In some cases, the role is split among different members of the district office staff. In one case, the entire management team served in the role of liaison. In districts with every school participating in the School Leadership Team Development Program, each team may identify a teacher as a liaison to the district. The teacher liaisons to the district may meet during each intersession with the superintendent and the assistant superintendent responsible to the schools. These meetings help to ensure that district support for the efforts of the team is well-targeted.

In many cases, the district has little experience with the processes, cultural norms, technical support, or skills necessary to engage in continuous improvement. The district liaison to the team or the team liaison to the district helps the district to understand, in specific, the work of the team and informs the district about the needs of the team. This information is critical to the district's learning and adjustment.

Selecting and Assigning Principals

Districts have begun to develop criteria for the selection of principals that include the candidates' capacity to work effectively with school leadership teams. Districts are seeking principals who have experience working on teams, have a philosophy of and propensity toward distributed leadership, and have confidence in teacher leadership.

Some districts have reconsidered a long-standing practice of routinely rotating principals. As they come to understand that a change in the makeup of a team, especially a change in principal, returns the team to its first stage of development, districts are questioning the wisdom of disrupting teams and are considering a more strategic and need-based approach to transferring principals.

Technical Support

Many districts find that the data routinely provided to schools by their information services are inadequate. Schools served by SLTs need more frequent and more various data than are typically available. Schools with monthly review and corrective action meetings, for example, need student data every thirty days. Districts and schools are challenged to provide staffing to support this data collection, format the data appropriately, and help teachers analyze the information. Reallocation of district and school resources is often necessary.

An SLT also needs detailed reports of standardized test data so that the team and the school staff can understand achievement patterns for subgroups of students. These reports add to the cost of standardized test reporting, making additional demands on school and district resources.

SLTs may also ask districts to provide information related to district benchmark assessments, such as writing, at frequent intervals and in specific formats. As teachers more closely and more frequently assess the impact of their instructional strategies, the demands on the system to provide results data increase. The district must be able to provide the necessary technical support.

Professional Development Support

Districts seeking to improve student achievement ask if their professional development is focused precisely on leadership and the improvement of instruction. In the past, too often a district's approach to professional development was to use training as a strategy to get disconnected initiatives launched from different departments of a Balkanized district office. In *Student Achievement Through Staff Development*, Bruce Joyce and Beverly Showers point out the pitfalls of a professional development program that lacks focus and suggest an alternative:

> *The effect of this kind of "shotgun" from the [district] office is to trivialize all of the initiatives. With only a few persons receiving relatively weak training in any one of them, the entire range of efforts simply evaporates in a short period of time.*
>
> *Such a diffused message simply confuses the schools that are disposed to cooperate and fuels the cynicism of those who are less disposed. The alternative is clear; the district...needs to screen initiatives and select only one or two for a major effort. (p. 22)*

Districts that work with the School Leadership Team Development Program, by definition, support professional development that is focused and coordinated. Furthermore, embedded within the continuous improvement planning process is a district approach to professional development that builds the leadership and instructional effectiveness not only of the system's teachers and staff, but also of its principals.

District Leadership Actions

Finally, district leaders committed to the School Leadership Team Development Program examine their own leadership behaviors. District leaders ask themselves the same question that Susan Rosenholtz poses in *Teachers' Workplace*, "whether those who administer districts are themselves models for how principals should treat their teachers, and teachers their students" (p. 172).

A Case in Point: Yuba City Unified School District

When Superintendent Willie Wong arrived in Yuba City a few years ago, he inherited a district with a large percentage of low-income minority students and a large number of underperforming schools. Wong found that the district's underperforming schools suffered more from a lack of vision than a lack of talent. He brought in CSLA with the idea of increasing student achievement in every school in the district.

One of CSLA's first recommendations was to build trust between school administrators and faculty. Getting principals into the classrooms on an informal basis was key, so CSLA devised the "3-minute walk-through." In contrast to formal 15-minute evaluation visits, the 3-minute walk-through was a chance for the principal to see more classrooms more often, to pick out key elements of instruction to discuss with teachers generally, and to build trust. Once administrators and staff were able to begin a free-flowing dialogue, CSLA advised the district to involve teachers in every aspect of the district's new academic vision.

This began with every school in the district establishing a school leadership team focused on improving student achievement. Every school revamped its annual academic plan and the SLT at each school helped teachers implement the new plan. Two years after beginning their work with CSLA, four of Yuba City's underperforming schools were eligible for large money rewards from the state. Since becoming partners with CSLA, the district's average Academic Performance Index has risen by more than 20 percent.

Wong attributes much of this improvement to the district's work with CSLA. "CSLA," he says, "is one of the most important aspects of developing effective schools because they focus not only on jump-starting your leadership program, but also on gaining the momentum to sustain it."

■ ■ ■ ■ ■

Chapter 4 Conclusion

In a decade of work with school leadership teams, the importance of district support for the teams has become increasingly clear to CSLA. Schools and their classrooms, the focal point of instructional change, exist within the larger system of the district. The relationship between the team and the district has a great influence on whether the district provides appropriate support. The district must have a clear understanding of what is required to support the continuous improvement of student achievement at the school level. The district must know the schools and the schools' contexts well. The district must help create a sense of structural tension, of urgency. It must also provide data. And it must offer professional development and resources to help resolve the structural tension. Some districts have made great progress. Other districts are coming to understand the leadership required to provide appropriate support.

Epilogue

The story of the work of school leadership teams is not complete. Other lessons wait to be written — lessons about ways to accelerate the work of teams and ways to focus on the needs of students more frequently and with keener precision. These yet unwritten lessons take into account the role of coaching support for principals and teams and the structuring of guided practice in leadership. The personal transformation that a team member undergoes as he or she develops into a leader is also a rich area for future exploration.

Robert Fritz's concept of "structural tension," referred to throughout, is another interesting area of focus. This book contains many references to leadership tools — tools that create structural tension and tools that resolve structural tension. If leadership is creating and then resolving an organization's structural tension, then knowing how to use these tools may be a promising approach to the future work of teams.

We are poised to apply all that we have learned from the past decade of work with school leadership teams to the issues and specific needs of low-performing schools. We anticipate serving an even larger proportion of chronically challenged schools in the future. Lessons about district support and the transitions involved in becoming a leader are likely to serve us well. So, too, will lessons about narrow focus and about support for the collaborative planning of curriculum and instruction. And the newly formed Network of Education Coaches, sponsored by CSLA, is able to provide high-quality coaching support to the team and the principal.

These possibilities are on the horizon, and it is our intention to publish any future lessons that we learn. With good fortune, we will not wait another decade to do so.

Appendices

Appendix A
CSLA Mission Statement

> To build leadership focused
> on teaching and learning
> so each and every student
> meets or exceeds standards.

CSLA Statement of Results

CSLA associates demonstrate leadership practices that guide and direct instructional improvement by

- creating culturally proficient schools intolerant of racism or exclusion
- facilitating the development, articulation, implementation, and stewardship of a vision of learning that is shared and supported by the school community
- advocating, nurturing, and sustaining a school culture and instructional program conducive to student learning and staff professional growth
- ensuring management of the organization, operations, and resources for a safe, efficient, and effective learning environment
- collaborating with families and community members, responding to diverse community interests and needs, and mobilizing community resources
- modeling a personal code of ethics and developing professional leadership capacity
- understanding, responding to, and influencing the larger political, social, economic, legal, and cultural context

The CSLA mission statement and statement of results were approved by consensus on March 9, 2001. They reflect the standards for education leaders adopted by the Interstate School Leaders Licensure Consortium (ISLLC) and CSLA's commitment to work toward them.

Appendix B

Results-Meeting Rubric: Implementation Stages

Data

Stage 1	Stage 2	Stage 3
■ Little or no student performance data are available at the meeting. ■ Discussion about student academic needs is subjective, speculative, unfocused, and based on opinion.	■ Student performance data are available, but incomplete. ■ Some of the data relate to standards and are relevant to the instructional program. ■ Evidence of data analysis is too superficial to be meaningful. ■ Data are not recent or are from annual assessment only.	■ Agreed-upon student performance data are collected and available at the meeting. ■ The data are standards-based and relevant to the instructional program. ■ Evidence of data analysis (e.g., charts, graphs, percentages) is available at the meeting. ■ Recent, periodic data are used.

Goals

Stage 1	Stage 2	Stage 3
■ Goals for improvement are not established, or are inappropriate (vague, unattainable, long-term). ■ There is no connection between student performance data and discussion of goals. ■ There is no agreement on a team goal.	■ Student achievement goals are somewhat vague or unrealistic, but viable if revised. ■ Goals tend to be annual, not short-term. ■ Goals are based on analysis of performance data. ■ Most members agree on the goal(s).	■ Student achievement goals are realistic, succinct, clear, and measurable. ■ Goals are short-term and attainable. ■ Performance data justify the goals. ■ There is agreement among the team members on the goals.

Strategies

Stage 1	Stage 2	Stage 3
■ Strategies do not relate to the goal(s) or assessment(s). ■ Strategies pertain to what others will do and focus on factors beyond the teachers' control. ■ Strategies are impossible to implement and unrealistic. ■ Obstacles to improvement are not identified or addressed. ■ There is no evaluation of previous strategies used.	■ Some strategies are relevant to the goals (assessments); others are not. ■ Most strategies describe what teachers/students will do. ■ Some strategies are specific, doable, and clearly written. ■ Most strategies are instructional and may address obstacles to improvement. ■ Successful strategies are identified, but are not all relevant to the goal.	■ Strategies are relevant to the goals (assessments). ■ Strategies state clearly what teachers/students will do. ■ Strategies are specific, doable, and clearly articulated. ■ Strategies are instructional and address obstacles to improvement. ■ Successful strategies are identified.

Teamwork

Stage 1	Stage 2	Stage 3
■ Members of the team work in isolation. ■ Focus of the team is on getting through the meeting. ■ Team members experience no growth in their knowledge of standards, curriculum, or teaching practices. ■ Group norms discourage team members from making contributions to the dialogue. ■ Individual personalities and predispositions dominate the meeting. ■ One or more members do not participate in the meeting.	■ Members' skills and experiences are utilized minimally. ■ Focus of the team is on compliance and relates to need to improve achievement. ■ Team members demonstrate increased interest in standards, curriculum, and teaching practices. ■ Dialogue among team members is polite and guarded. ■ Members attempt to monitor their own personalities and predispositions in the interest of the team's effective functioning. ■ Dominant members sometimes control the meetings.	■ Members' complementary skills and experiences are shared. ■ Focus of the team is on goal attainment. ■ Team members' skilled implementation of standards, curriculum, and teaching practices is evident. ■ Dialogue among the team members is purposeful and professional. ■ Individual personalities and predispositions do not drive the meetings. ■ All members of the team contribute during the meetings.

Process

Stage 1	Stage 2	Stage 3
■ Meetings are held infrequently and sporadically. ■ Meetings are unplanned, aimless, and too brief or too long. ■ Focus of the meetings is unclear to the team members (Why are we doing this?). ■ There is no record of the meeting; team members take no responsibility for action. ■ Success is not experienced, acknowledged, or celebrated.	■ Meetings are routinely scheduled, but held too infrequently. ■ Time during meetings is not always used in a productive manner; planning for meetings is minimal; there is an agenda. ■ Goal attainment is generally understood to be the purpose of the meetings. ■ Notes from the meetings are recorded and usually distributed; the team consents to implement the plan. ■ Success is based on data, sometimes acknowledged, and celebrated by team members only.	■ Meetings are routinely scheduled and continuous. ■ Meetings are planned, facilitated, and time efficient. ■ Focus of the meetings is on attainment of the goal. ■ A record of the meeting (action plan) is distributed to all team members; the team is committed to implementing the plan. ■ Success is supported by data, acknowledged, and celebrated publicly.

Results-Meeting Rubric: Implementation Self-Assessment

Place yourself on the continuum, using an X to indicate where you are in the implementation process for each area:

Component	Stage 1	Stage 2	Stage 3
Data	o————————————o		
Notes:			
Goals	o————————————o		
Notes:			
Strategies	o————————————o		
Notes:			
Teamwork	o————————————o		
Notes:			
Process	o————————————o		
Notes:			

This rubric and self-assessment were developed by Phillip Perez, Deputy Superintendent, Riverside Unified School District, based on information from *Results: The Key to Continuous School Improvement*, by Mike Schmoker. Used with permission.

Appendix C

Agreements for Effective Collaborative Work between the North Bay School Leadership Center and _____ Unified School District School Leadership Teams and Site Principals

The role of the North Bay School Leadership Center will be to...	The role of the District Office will be to...
■ assist the school team to "engage the school community in creating the technical and cultural conditions in which teachers continually improve curriculum, instruction, and assessment practices, resulting in individual student achievement." The School Leadership Center, the District Office, and school sites will establish specific measures to evaluate progress; e.g., SAT 9 (API). ■ provide qualified trainers/facilitators for all seminars. ■ provide feedback to district office and support personnel. ■ provide coaching to SLT principals to assist them in meeting school and personal professional goals. ■ will schedule facilities for all SLT trainings. ■ provide all training materials. ■ provide morning refreshments and lunch for all participants.	■ provide evidence of support from the superintendent and the board of trustees for the work of the School Leadership Team and the implementation of their improvement plan; provide release time for teachers and principals. ■ provide a description of how the district office will support and participate in the School Leadership Team process. ■ make clear the decision-making authority of the principals and the School Leadership Team. ■ support the development of clear and measurable student achievement performance goals for each school. ■ establish personal professional development goals for each principal.

The role of the School Leadership Team will be to...	The role of the Principals will be to....
■ provide a description of how the School Leadership Team will engage the staff and community in the continuous improvement system. ■ provide a description of how the School Leadership Team will inform and engage the collective bargaining agent in the work of the School Leadership Team. ■ provide evidence of consensus within the team that supports the School Leadership Team's shared purpose. A statement of purpose has been written and communicated to the school community. School Leadership Team goals will focus on student achievement as indicated by measurable criteria. ■ provide evidence of how time will be allocated to enable the school to accomplish their student achievement goals. ■ participate in all School Leadership Team trainings. ■ complete agreed upon tasks between School Leadership Team meetings.	■ lead the development of a site plan which addresses components of continuous improvement planning, including goals, use of data, assessment, and staff development. ■ work with the district office support staff to establish personal professional development goals. ■ schedule time for personal coaching with the North Bay School Leadership Center personnel. ■ participate in all School Leadership Team trainings with team. ■ allocate time to work with School Leadership Team during intersession.

North Bay School Leadership Center

_____
Unified School District

School Name

_____

Bob Pape,
Executive Director

Superintendent

Site Principal

SLT Members

Gail Wright, Director,
Program Delivery

District Liaison

_____

_____

District Liaison

_____

_____

_____

_____

Date of Agreement

_____

Appendix D
School Leadership Team Program
Impact Questionnaire

Team Consensus

School: _____   Region: _____

Directions: Please work as a team to discuss and come to an agreement about the impact of the team's work this year. The team's discussion should result in a consensus response to each question. Thank you!

1. **Focus on the SAT 9**
    What work has the team done this year to address SAT 9 issues?

    What did you learn/do in the SLT sessions that helped with this work?

2. **Focus on Student Learning (other than SAT 9 preparation)**
    Describe two major activities of the SLT this year that have made a difference in the lives and learning of students. (Include a statement of supporting evidence.)

    Description of Activity One:

    Evidence of Impact:

    Description of Activity Two:

    Evidence of Impact:

    What did you learn/do in the SLT sessions that helped with these activities?

3. **Focus on Engaging the Rest of the Staff**

    Describe in detail two major activities of the SLT this year that have strengthened working relations among staff members. (Be sure to include a statement of supporting evidence.)

    Description of Activity One:

    Evidence of Impact:

    Description of Activity Two:

    Evidence of Impact:

    What did you learn/do in the SLT sessions that helped with these activities?

4. **Focus on the Team**

    How would you describe our leadership team's development?

    What did you learn/do in the SLT sessions that helped with this development?

5. **Focus on the District**

    What support and assistance have the district provided to help the SLT do its work?

Appendix E

School Leadership Team Implementation Continuum: Individual Team Member Form

About This Survey

This survey was developed by the SLT research team at the University of California, Santa Barbara, Gervitz Graduate School of Education, with extensive input from the California School Leadership Academy regional directors. Based on an analysis of teams' responses over the last four years, we have modified the survey to address the development and evolution of the SLT program. The survey has been designed as a rubric to capture the complex process of the SLT program and its goals for the team, for schoolwide change, and for student learning.

Research on school change informs us that change often begins with the individual, before it progresses to the school as a whole. Therefore, in most instances, this SLT Implementation Continuum starts with the individual and then describes various levels of team or whole school activity. If, for many of these categories, you believe your team is at the individual or beginning levels, that is a valued response.

The categories are based on the information from the SLT program description, which outlines expected outcomes and performance indicators. We realize that not all teams are at the same place. Some teams have only completed one year of the SLT program. In addition, not all teams have had the same SLT program content since implementation of the program is a locally negotiated decision. Therefore, there are no right or wrong answers. Responses to this survey represent a snapshot of where you perceive your team to be *right now.*

All responses from individuals will remain anonymous. Any reports and/or publications resulting from this study will not identify schools by name, but school names are needed to be able to provide data back to each team.

The success of this project is strengthened by the time, thought, and candor that each team member contributes to it. We appreciate your contributions and are committed to treating them with respect and care.

The Benefits

All data collected from the team will be reported back to the team for its own use. The time, energy, and concentration you give to completing this survey will provide helpful information to your own school and the CSLA state and regional directors, as well as helping to expand our general knowledge of the challenges of leading schoolwide change.

Directions for Individual Team Members

1. Read through the responses to each category and then bubble in on the Individual Team Member Response Form the response that most accurately or typically reflects your team *from your perspective*. The response form will be computer read. *Please use a black pen, felt tip if possible.*

2. Do not spend too much time on any one item or category. Your first reaction is sufficient.

3. This task should take about 20 minutes.

School Leadership Team Implementation Continuum:
Individual Team Member Form

Category	1	2	3	4	5
1. SLT team relationships	Individual team members are aware of team-building skills presented in the SLT seminars, but the team has not yet applied these skills to create a cohesive team.	Team members are trying to openly discuss issues, deal with conflicts, and establish processes for solving problems and making decisions.	Team members are able to engage in honest and open discussion, and the team is identifying key issues it wants to address.	The SLT is coalescing into an effective working and problem-solving team, and together is pursuing clear goals.	The SLT is effectively using its problem-solving and group process skills to engage staff in accomplishing its goals.
2. SLT team to staff relationship	Most staff members are unaware of who is serving on the SLT, and the team's work is not shared with the staff.	The school staff knows who serves on the SLT team, but not everyone supports or understands the purpose of the SLT.	The SLT team actively shares its work with the staff and is generally supported by the staff.	The SLT engages with most of the staff between SLT seminars, shares what it is learning, and involves the staff.	The entire staff values the SLT's work and relies on the team's leadership to guide school improvement work.
3. SLT team to other school groups	The SLT team does not interact with other official school committees.	Some SLT team members also serve on other committees and informally share information.	There is regular, formal communication between the team and other school committees.	Joint planning meetings are held with other school committees.	The SLT team collaborates with other school committees to achieve continuous improvement.
4. SLT team to district communi-cations	The district has given written or tacit approval, but there is no communication between district personnel and the SLT about SLT activities.	A district liaison is assigned to the school, but there is limited interaction between the liaison and the SLT team.	A district liaison regularly meets with the SLT team to assist its efforts and may be an active team member.	The district liaison and the SLT work together to resolve issues that may impede the continuous improvement process.	There is regular communication among the liaison, the SLT, and the district staff, which ensures coordination and maximizing of improvement efforts.

School Leadership Team Implementation Continuum:
Individual Team Member Form *(continued)*

Category	1	2	3	4	5
5. District support for the SLT work	The SLT feels little support from the district for its work to improve student learning.	The SLT receives financial support to attend SLT seminars.	The SLT and the district are exploring ways for the district to increase its support for the SLT's work.	The district and the SLT team collaborate to identify strategies and resources to improve student learning.	Through the SLT's work, the district rethinks or develops new policies and practices and allocates resources to facilitate the work.
6. SLT/district account-ability	The SLT team operates in compliance with district policies and guidelines, but there is little interaction in relation to district and school goals.	The SLT team has discussed the relationship between school and district goals.	The SLT team's action plans, the school's goals, and the district's goals focus on improving student learning.	The district, school, and SLT feel their goals for students are in alignment and there is a growing sense of shared accountability for student learning.	The school, with SLT leadership, and district share equally in their accountability for student learning and work together to achieve the goal of continuous improvement.
7. Principal to SLT/staff relationship	The principal is not a regular member of the team.	The principal attends SLT meetings regularly.	The principal and team are developing a collegial working relationship.	The principal and the SLT are able to sustain a productive working relationship even when problems arise.	The principal and the SLT work together to redefine the school as a community of leaders and learners.
8. Norms of collaboration	SLT members interact based on informal and unwritten rules of conduct during team meetings, which may change in different situations.	SLT members discuss the need for norms or rules of conduct for team meetings and agree to follow them.	The SLT agrees on the norms for healthy group work and consequences for not following the norms.	The SLT works with the whole staff to reach consensus on norms and consequences, which they use when working together.	Staff and community members routinely refer to the school's norms and hold each other accountable for healthy, active group participation.

School Leadership Team Implementation Continuum:
Individual Team Member Form *(continued)*

Category	1	2	3	4	5
9. Capacity building	SLT team members are aware that the team needs the capacity to lead the school.	SLT team members are able to be leaders in their classrooms and in other roles beyond the classroom as a result of SLT participation.	The SLT team is coalescing as a leadership group in the school by sharing with others what it is learning.	The SLT team is playing an active leadership role in guiding schoolwide change and expanding the definition and scope of leadership.	The SLT team helps other stakeholders develop leadership capacity for the process of continuous school improvement.
10. Using data to inform action (e.g., inquiry cycle, continuous improvement cycle, action research)	SLT members have not been introduced to the concepts of using data to inform action as an integral part of a cycle of continuous improvement.	The SLT is discussing the concepts of using data as an integral part of a cycle of continuous improvement and understand how data can inform action.	The SLT is developing specific plans for the collection and analysis of data to monitor implementation of selected strategies and their impact on student achievement.	The SLT occasionally involves the staff in collecting and analyzing student achievement data in order for the staff to take informed actions.	The SLT frequently and regularly involves the staff in collecting and analyzing student achievement data in order for the staff to take informed actions.
11. Communication	There is little or no communication among SLT team members between SLT seminars.	The SLT team meets and communicates about SLT business at least once between seminars.	The SLT meets regularly and gets feedback about SLT work from others in the school community.	The SLT meets regularly and has multiple processes for open communication within the school community.	There are excellent ongoing processes and multiple channels for open communication between the SLT and the entire school community.
12. Shared vision for powerful and continuous learning and improvement	Individual SLT team members hold a vision about what needs to change for continuous learning and improvement, but do not share it with others.	SLT team members share and discuss their individual visions of continuous learning and are building a common vision.	SLT team members are developing the team's vision of continuous learning, and they ask critical questions about individual and schoolwide practices.	SLT team and the total school community are collaboratively developing their vision of learning, and they are asking critical questions about schoolwide practices.	The schoolwide vision of continuous learning and improvement guides schoolwide actions as evidenced by improved performance by students and adults.

School Leadership Team Implementation Continuum:
Individual Team Member Form (continued)

Category	1	2	3	4	5
13. Learning environment that supports diversity	SLT team members are aware of the need to create diversity-sensitive learning environments.	SLT members use new knowledge to create diversity-sensitive environments in their own classrooms.	SLT team discusses how to create diversity-sensitive classroom environments within the school.	SLT is leading the staff in discussing and planning diversity-sensitive learning environments.	The school community values a diversity-sensitive learning environment; these values guide design of all classroom and school interactions.
14. Curriculum design and setting standards	Individual SLT team members do not fully understand the concept of a standards-based curriculum; the curriculum is designed around available materials and what individual teachers think students need to know.	Individual SLT team members understand the general concepts of a standards-based curriculum and are identifying work to be done specific to the school's achievement goal.	The SLT is discussing and planning for schoolwide implementation of a standards-based curriculum and benchmarks or indicators related to the school's selected achievement goals.	The SLT is facilitating schoolwide discussion about and planning for the implementation of a standards-based curriculum and benchmarks or indicators related to the school's selected achievement goals.	The SLT is facilitating the staff and community engagement in the implementation of a standards-based curriculum and benchmarks or indicators related to the school's selected achievement goals.
15. Evaluation of student work	SLT team members individually review their own students' work to assess student success and plan instruction.	SLT team members are aware of the importance of collaboratively reviewing student work as part of a process of continuous learning and improvement.	As a team, SLT members are collaboratively reviewing student work from several age and ability levels to find ways of strengthening teaching and learning.	SLT team members are helping other staff members (e.g., in grade-level teams or departments) to review and reflect on student work across school levels to find ways of strengthening teaching and learning.	Staff, students, and community regularly engage in reflecting on student work to guide curriculum and to strengthen teaching and assessment strategies that lead to continuous improvement.

School Leadership Team Implementation Continuum:
Individual Team Member Form (continued)

Category	1	2	3	4	5
16. Working from research and data	Individual SLT team members are reading and using relevant research about powerful learning and school change.	The SLT team discusses relevant education research and is collecting data to inform its decisions.	The SLT team members share their research readings and data with other members of the school community informally.	The SLT team is formally sharing research and data with the whole school (e.g., presentation at a staff meeting, staff development day).	The staff and community are reading, discussing, and using research and data to drive school improvement on a continuous basis.
17. Working with student assessment and other outcome measures	Individual SLT team members are familiar with and use student assessment data.	The SLT team is collecting and reviewing a variety of student assessment and achievement data.	The SLT team is actively using student achievement and assessment data (including student work) to set goals and develop action plans.	The SLT works with staff to understand the importance of student achievement data (including student work) to analyze programs and make decisions.	Staff and community collect, analyze, and use student achievement data, especially student work, to improve teaching and learning.
18. Assessing standards-based teaching and learning	SLT members possess some knowledge of standards-based teaching and learning and criteria that could be used to assess it.	The SLT team discusses the differences between current practice and standards-based teaching and learning; criteria for assessing it are being explored by the team.	The SLT team initiates discussions with staff members about standards-based teaching and learning and is exploring criteria for assessing it in classrooms.	Through the SLT leadership, staff and community understand what is standards-based student work and the SLT team is establishing assessment criteria.	Staff and community establish local criteria and instruments to assess the degree to which students are achieving standards. These are used to guide continuous improvement.
19. Going to scale	Individual team members are using what they are learning from SLT training in their respective roles.	The team as a whole uses the information from SLT seminars to bring about change (e.g., development of a pilot project).	SLT team members are working with other staff members, parents, or students to use information from SLT seminars to bring about change.	As a result of SLT team leadership, many staff members, parents, and students are actively involved in continuous school improvement.	Staff and community engage in continuous efforts to create a powerful learning environment for all that respects diversity and multicultural understanding.

Appendix F
Documenting Team Progress and Learnings

"Fill-in-as-You-Go Implementation Story"

*What actually happened at*_____

Documentation Areas		
Major Events & Intersession Activities		
Results		
Learnings & Best Practices		
Artifacts for the SLT Portfolio		

Adapted from Suzanne Bailey (2000). *Making Progress Visible: Implementing Standards and Other Large-Scale Change Initiatives*, p. 67. Vacaville, Calif.: Bailey Alliance. Used with permission.

References

Arbuckle, Margaret A., and Lynn B. Murray. *Building Systems for Professional Growth: An Action Guide*. Andover, Mass.: The Regional Laboratory for Educational Improvement of the Northeast and Islands and the Maine Department of Educational and Cultural Services, 1989.

Bailey, Suzanne. *Making Progress Visible: Implementing Standards and Other Large-Scale Change Initiatives*. Vacaville, Calif.: Bailey Alliance, 2000.

Barth, Roland S. *Learning by Heart*. San Francisco: Jossey-Bass Publishers, 2001.

———. "Teacher Leader," *Phi Delta Kappan*, vol. 82, no. 6, February 2001, pp. 443–49.

Brown, S., and K. Eisenhardt. *Competing on the Edge*. Boston: Harvard Business School Press, 1998.

Chrispeels, Janet H., Janet H. Brown, Joyce Wang, Kathleen J. Martin, and Cheryl Strait. "California School Leadership Teams: Building Capacity for School Change." Gervitz Graduate School of Education, University of California, Santa Barbara, August 28, 1998.

Chrispeels, Janet H., Salvador Castillo, and Janet Brown. "School Leadership Teams: A Process Model." Gervitz Graduate School of Education, University of California, Santa Barbara, July 1997.

———. "School Leadership Teams: A Process Model of Team Development." Gervitz Graduate School of Education, University of California, Santa Barbara, June 1999.

Costa, Arthur L., and Robert J. Garmston. *Cognitive Coaching: A Foundation for Renaissance Schools, Syllabus,* 4th ed. Highlands Ranch, Colo.: Center for Cognitive Coaching, 1999.

Council of Chief State School Officers. *Interstate School Leaders Licensure Consortium: Standards for School Leaders*. Washington, DC: Council of Chief State School Officers, 1996.

Deal, Terrence E., and Kent D. Peterson. *Shaping School Culture: The Heart of Leadership*. San Francisco: Jossey-Bass Publishers, 1999.

Deming, W. Edwards. *Out of the Crisis*. Cambridge: MIT Press, 1986.

Drucker, Peter F. *The Effective Executive*. New York: Harper and Row, 1976.

Earl, L., and L. Lee. *School Improvement: What Have We Learned from the Manitoba Experience?* Toronto: Walter and Duncan Gordon Foundation, 1998.

Edmonds, R. "Some Schools Work and More Can." *Journal of Social Policy,* March/April, 1979, pp. 28–32.

Elmore, Richard F. *Building a New Structure for School Leadership*. Washington, DC: The Albert Shanker Institute, Winter 2000.

Evans, Robert. *The Human Side of School Change: Reform, Resistance, and the Real-Life Problems of Innovation*. San Francisco: Jossey-Bass Publishers, 1996.

Fritz, Robert. *The Path of Least Resistance: Designing Organizations to Succeed*. New York: Ballantine Books, Random House, 1989.

Fullan, Michael. *Change Forces*. New York: The Falmer Press, 1993.

———. "Leadership for the 21st Century: Breaking the Bonds of Dependency." *Educational Leadership,* vol. 55, no. 7, April 1998, pp. 6–10.

———. *Change Forces: The Sequel*. New York: The Falmer Press, 1999.

Fullan, Michael G., with Suzanne Stiegelbauer. *The New Meaning of Educational Change*. New York: Teachers College Press, 1991.

Geiser, Kristin Donaldson, and Paul Berman, with Sofia Aburto, John Ericson, Nancy Kamprath, Akili Moses, Beryl Nelson, Debra Silverman, Haleh Sprehe, Victoria Thorp, and Aurora Wood. *Building Implementation Capacity for Continuous Improvement*. Emeryville, Calif.: RPP International, September 2000.

Hopkins, D. *A Teacher's Guide to Classroom Research*. Buckingham: Open University Press, 1993.

Joyce, Bruce, and Beverly Showers. *Student Achievement Through Staff Development*. White Plains, N.Y.: Longman, 1988.

Joyce, Bruce, James Wolf, and Emily Calhoun. *The Self-Renewing School*. Alexandria, Va.: Association for Supervision and Curriculum Development, 1993.

Lambert, Linda. *Building Leadership Capacity in Schools*. Alexandria, Va.: Association for Supervision and Curriculum Development, 1998.

Lein, Laura, Joseph F. Johnson Jr., and Mary Ragland (primary authors). "Successful Texas Schoolwide Programs: Research Study Results," in *Schoolwide Programs and High-Performing, High-Poverty Schools: A Collection of Articles from the STAR Center*. Austin, Tex.: Charles A. Dana Center, University of Texas at Austin, 1997.

Lieberman, Ann, and Lynne Miller. *Teachers — Transforming Their World and Their Work*. New York: Teachers College Press, 1999.

Marsh, D., J. McMahon, B. Pahre, and J. Sevilla. *School Principals as Instructional Leaders: The Impact of the California School Leadership Academy*. Los Angeles: University of Southern California, 1990.

Rosenholtz, Susan J. *Teachers' Workplace*. New York: Teachers College Press, 1989.

Schmoker, Mike. *Results: The Key to Continuous School Improvement*. Alexandria, Va.: Association for Supervision and Curriculum Development, 1996.

———. "Results: The Essential Elements." Presentation at California School Leadership Academy convocation, Burlingame, Calif., January 17, 1998.

———. "Results: The Key to Continuous School Improvement," in California School Leadership Academy. *Standards and Accountability: The Substance of Leadership*. Hayward, Calif.: California School Leadership Academy, 1998.

Senge, Peter. *The Fifth Discipline*. New York: Doubleday, 1990.

Senge, Peter M., Art Kleiner, Charlotte Roberts, Richard B. Ross, and Bryan J. Smith. *The Fifth Discipline Fieldbook: Strategies and Tools for Building a Learning Organization*. New York: Currency, Doubleday, 1994.

Thompson, Steven R. "Site-Based Development," in *Professional Development in Learning-Centered Schools*, ed. Sarah DeJarnette Caldwell. Oxford, Ohio: National Staff Development Council, 1997, pp. 12–33.

WestEd. *Moving Leadership Standards into Everyday Work*. San Francisco: WestEd, 2003.